Our Tennessee Mountain Home

Olivia Helton Crisp

Robcan International Publishers
1941 Bluff Mountain Road
Sevierville, Tennessee 37876 7335

Table of Contents

Our Tennessee Mountain Home

Foreword

There are three things that one should hold dear in life. Faith, family and friends. When I was approached by a dear friend about helping with putting this book project together, I was overjoyed to see such heartwarming information and stories as well as old photographs and newspaper clippings which flooded my own mind with "precious memories." Life is a continuous story from birth until death. There are good times as well as bad times. It is human nature I suppose to attempt to keep a record of both. Remembering helps us to rejoice, laugh, grieve and at the same time learn to live and cope with whatever life brings our way. Life in general is filled with the known and unknown. When one is surrounded with people like those you will meet in this book, all of life's uncertainties, surprises, knowns and unknowns can be met with the understanding that whatever life has to offer, it is worth living. Having the privilege of helping to bring this book to fruition is not only an honor but a blessing to me personally. I have known this family all of my life which makes me feel like a part of the story also. The people of East Tennessee and the Great Smoky Mountains area in particular are usually close knit in every aspect of life. Faith, family and friends help each of us to rejoice in our blessings, share in our burdens, and comfort when we suffer loss. I began this project knowing that as the pages come together I am in the midst of a balancing act between publishing and releasing music worldwide, preparing to do music soundtracks and songs for an up coming family film and movie to be filmed in the Smoky Mountains area, publishing a series of children's books titled "Frog Hollow," and at the same time doing my classes with Harvard University. But in spite of all that, as you read through the following pages, remember, "Our Tennessee Mountain Home" is more than words on paper, it is life as we know it.

Dr. Robert Freeman Ownby
Harvard University -Harvard Law School.

This book is more than just about genealogy.

The author lives within sight of her childhood home. She has included some interesting personal stories, facts about mountain living and little-known information about the area from old newspaper articles, stories, and photographs.

It provides a rare glimpse into Smoky Mountain living from a true native to the area.

The love of a
FAMILY
is life's greatest blessing

THE CRISP FAMILY

Crisp Family Photo

Top Row: Lucy, Wilma Jean, Bethel and Ray. Bottom Row seated: Juanita, Anna Jo, Alice Crisp, Claude Crisp and Junior.

"I am the nation"

I was born on July 4, 1776, and the Declaration of
  Independence is my birth certificate.
The bloodlines of the world run in my veins, because
  I offered freedom to the oppressed.
I am many things and many people.

                    I am the nation.

I am 200 million living souls and the ghost of
  Millions who have lived and died for me.
I am Nathan Hale and Paul Revere. I stood at
  Lexington and fired the shot heard around the world.
I am Washington, Jefferson, and Patrick Henry.
  I am John Paul Jones, the Green Mountain Boys, and
  Davy Crockett.

I am Lee and Grant and Abe Lincoln. I remember the
  Alamo, the Maine, and Pearl Harbor.
When freedom called I answered, and stayed until
  It was over, over there.
I left my heroic dead in Flanders' Field, on the
  Rock of Corregidor, on the bleak slopes of Korea,
And in the steaming jungles of Vietnam.

I am the Brooklyn Bridge, the wheat lands of Kansas,
  And the granite hills of Vermont.
I am the coal fields of the Virginias and Pennsylvania;
  The fertile lands of the West, the Golden Gate, and
The Grand Canyon. I am Independence Hall, the
  Monitor, and the Merrimac.

I am big. I sprawl from the Atlantic to the Pacific.
  My arms reach out to embrace Alaska and Hawaii . . .
Three million square miles throbbing with industry.
  I am more than five million farms. I am forest,
  field, mountain, and desert.
I am quiet villages and cities that never sleep.

You can look at me and see Ben Franklin walking down
  The streets of Philadelphia with his breadloaf under
  his arm. You can see Betsy Ross with her needle.
You can see the lights of Christmas and hear the
  Strains of "Auld Lang Syne" as the calendar turns.

I am Babe Ruth and the World Series.
  I am 130,000 schools and colleges.
I am 320,000 churches where my people worship
  God as they think best.
I am a ballot dropped in a box, the roar of a crowd
  In a stadium, and the voices of a choir in a cathedral.
I am an editorial in a newspaper and a letter to a
  Congressman.
I am Albert Einstein and Billy Graham.

I am Eli Whitney and Stephen Foster and Tom Edison.
  I am Horace Greeley, Will Rogers, and the Wright
Brothers. I am George Washington Carver, Daniel
  Webster, and Jonas Salk. I am Longfellow, Harriet
Beecher Stowe, Walt Whitman, and Thomas Paine.

Yes, I am the nation, and these are the things that I am.
  I was conceived in freedom and, God willing, in
Freedom I will spend the rest of my days.

May I possess always the integrity, the courage, and the
  Strength to keep myself unshackled, to remain a
Citadel of freedom and a beacon of hope to the world.

By Otto Whittaker

My husband Bethel Crisp's mother and father met and married in Proctor, North Carolina, September 25, 1918.

His dad went there to work for the Ritter Lumber Company. His mom went there with her sister Zora and her husband Bill Gilland. Bill worked on the train. Bethel's uncle Rob Crisp also worked on the train and got caught between two box cars and was killed. He was taken back to Andrews, North Carolina and buried in the Valley Town Cemetery.

In 1943 the Tennessee Valley Authority a quasi governmental agency took the homes, communities and livelihoods of those in a 44,000 acre area of Swain and Graham Counties. World War II was on and the government said it needed to flood the land to build a lake and a dam. The dam would provide electricity to make aluminum for the war effort.

According to information provided by North Carolina Congressman Charles Taylor. The average price received by families for compensation was $6.00 per acre while the average market price for undeveloped land at that time was nearly $37.00 an acre. Proctor was located on Hazel Creek about 20 miles as the crow flies, over the mountain to Cades Cove. It is now officially referred to as Backcountry Campsite 86, GSMNP.

As part of its flood control plan, T.V.A. annually draws down Fontana Lake, which has a peak elevation of 1,710 feet. Every 5 years T.V.A. has to draw the lake down by 145 feet to inspect and repair the 480 foot high dam.

Congressman Taylor assured people that a road would be built from Bryson City along the North Shore to access the cemeteries of families who had to move.

Work began on the road but ceased after about 9 miles due to environmental issues. It is now referred to as the "Road to Nowhere." Mildred Cable Johnson and others who have families buried in the cemetery have kept the graves and grounds in honor of their ancestors for years.

Cemetery Decorations are in May each year

UP AND RUNNING: The saw mill and mill pond at Proctor, a community of about 1,000 before it was flooded when Fontana reservoir was constructed in 1943.

The Family Lineage of Bethel Crisp-Father and Mother

Bethel's father was Claude Ernest Crisp born September 27, 1899. Claude is the son of James Monroe Crisp and Louise Elizabeth Phillips of Andrews, North Carolina. They are buried in the Valleytown Cemetery, Andrews, North Carolina.

Their Children: #1. Robert Crisp who married Helen. They had four children Hubert "Hub," Tommy, Katherine, and Helen. Robert Crisp was killed in a train accident in Proctor North Carolina. They brought his body back and buried him in Valleytown Cemetery in Andrews, North Carolina.

#2. Grace, who married Oslo Pullium had a son, Frank and two other sons.

 Second marriage? Lawson, no children.

#3. Sister Nora who married Bob McClelland. They have four children: Mary, Buster, James and Lee.

Bethel's Mother's Family.

 Alice Roxie Ogle Crisp born July 2 , 1900 In Tennessee.

Alice is the daughter of David Ogle born July 22, 1864.

Lucy Cole Born October 11, 1867. David Ogle and Lucy Cole were married October 11, 1885. They had four daughters. #1 Elizabeth "Lizzy," born March 14, 1887, #2 Martha Lzora, born March 29, 1891, #3 Maude May born January 5, 1898. #4 Alice Roxie, born July 2, 1900.

 Lucy Cole Ogle died giving birth to another child. She and the child were buried in the foothills of the Great Smoky Mountains in North Carolina. Lucy was later took up and reburied in Bryson City, North Carolina.

 David Ogle brought his four daughters, Elizabeth, Martha, Maude and Alice across the Great Smoky Mountains to live in Gatlinburg, Tennessee. There he met and married Etta Brackins and had six more children. #1 Thad, #2 Velma, #3 Hansel, #4 Carl, #5 Kate and #6 Dortha Lee.

 David Ogle and Etta Brackins Family.

#1 Thad Ogle. Never married.

#2 Velma. Married Luther Ward and had five children. #1 Reba, #2 J. L., #3 Oscar Dee, #4 Buddy Lee, #5 Mary Louise.

Hansil (#3) married Dorothy Huskey and had six children. #1 Joyce, #2 Jim, #3 Bob, #4 Debby, #5 Patsy, #6 Connie.

Carl (#4) married Dorothy Huskey and had three children. #1 J.D., #2 Evelyn, #3 Helen.

5, Kate married Robert Huskey and had three children. #1 Mary, #2 Barbara, #3 Roberta.

#6 Dorothy Lee married Virgil Latham. They had three children. #1 Johnny, #2 Billy, #3 Virginia. Bethel's grandpa, David Ogle was the first man to be buried in the Mountain View Missionary Baptist Church Cemetery. He was licensed to preach by Mountain View Baptist Church.

Bethel's father and mother, Claude Ernest Crisp and Alice Roxie Ogle Crisp met and married in Proctor, North Carolina September 25th 1918 by reverend Joseph Hayes. Their children are Lucy, James, Bethel, Anna Jo, Ray, Juanita, Wilma Jean and Claude Junior.

#1 Lucy Elizabeth, born may 6, 1920 at Hazel Creek, North Carolina, married Max Phillips of Andrews, North Carolina. No children. Second marriage, to Charles Morgan

Blairsville, Georgia. Third marriage, Chuck Love. No children.

Lucy died October 14, 1990 in Atlanta, Georgia of cancer. She is buried in the Valleytown Cemetery Andrews, North Carolina.

#2 James David Crisp, born July 25, 1924, Andrews North Carolina. Entered the U.S. Army April 7, 1943, Camp Mackall, North Carolina. Serving as a one of the Glider Infantry Regiment, he was killed in Belgium, January 7,

1945, World War II. James was buried there, then after the war was over they brought him to Andrews, North Carolina and buried him in the Valleytown Cemetery.

#3 Bethel Chandler Crisp, born November 7, 1925 in East Laport, North Carolina. Married Olivia Ellender Helton, October 9, 1947, had three sons, (1) James William Crisp, born July 28, 1948. Married Paulette Williamson of Walland, Tennessee.

(2) Howard Donald Crisp, born August 9, 1949. Married Barbara Garner, they had one child, Jennifer Louise Crisp. They are now divorced. Howard's second marriage was to Carolyn McBee. Jennifer Louise married Mark Christianer. They had two children, Devin Caleb and Chase Wesley Christianer Jennifer and Mark are divorced. Jennifer Louise died January 31, 2008, age 38 of leukemia. She is buried in the Mountain View Baptist Church cemetery.

(3) Joe Ernest Crisp, born February 18, 1955. Married Sherry Justus. Two children, Justin Ernest, married Jewelle Bickel; Olivia Jean, married William Lakatosh.

#4 Anna Jo Crisp, born January 11, 1928 Smokemont, North Carolina. Died April 1, 1988, married Hubert (Hub) Crisp. They have a daughter Janet Diane who died young and Daniel Herbert Crisp, he is married to Gail and lives in the Florida Keys.

Second marriage to Herman Nelson. Divorced. Third marriage to Monroe Nelson. She died April 1, 1988. Anna Jo is buried in Valleytown Cemetery Andrews, North Carolina.

#5 Bobby Ray Crisp, born August 9, 1930 at Bryson City, North Carolina. Married to Evelyn Marie Adams, August 5 1950. Their six children are: Anita Gwen, Juanita Ray,

Bobby Ray Jr., William Claude, Adam Wayne, Elizabeth Kit.

#6 Juanita Elzora, born June 5, 1934 in Glamorgan Virginia. Married Robert Kilpatrick. They had four children, John, Allen, Karen and Robin. Robin married Jim Allen. They have one child, Jim Allen Jr. Allen married Ava.

#7 Wilma Jean, born June 8 1937, Norton, Virginia. Married Joe Owens December 23, 1960. Two children, Kathy (married with one child, Jacob), Melissa Owens.

#8 Claude Ernest Crisp Jr. Born May 31, 1942, Wise Virginia. Married Carolyn Marie Nichols July 8, 1963, Robbinsville, North Carolina. Children are Brian Claude. Born May 3, 1964, Richard Deion. Born January 24, 1968, Jason and Nichole.

{Some people come into our lives, make footprints on our hearts and we are never the same.}

That Old Ragged Flag

I walked through a County Court House square
On a a park bench an old man was sitting there.
I said, "Your old Court House is kinda run down."
He said, "No, it will do in our little town."
I said, "Your old flag pole is leaning a little bit.
And that's a ragged old Flag you've got hanging on it."
He said, "Have a seat" and I sat down.
"Is this the first time you've been to our little town?"
I said, "I think it is."
"Well," he said. "I don't like to brag but we're kinda proud of that
ragged old flag.
You see, we got a little hole in that flag there, when Washington
took it across the Delaware.
And, it got powder burns, the night Francis Scott Key sat
watching it, writing 'Oh Say Can You See.'
And it got a bad rip at New Orleans

When Packingham, and Jackson took it on the scene.
And, it almost fell at the Alamo beside the Texas flag;
But, she waved on through, until
She got cut with a sword at Chancellorsville,
And she got cut again at Shiloh Hill.
There was Robert E. Lee, Beauregard, and Bragg,
The south wind blew hard on that ragged old Flag.
On Flander's Field in World War One
She got a big hole from a Bertha gun.
She turned blood red in World War Two
And she hung limp and low a time or two.
She was in Korea and Vietnam,
She went where she was sent by her Uncle Sam.
She waved from our ships on the briny foam,
Now they've about quit waving her back here at home.
In our good land here she's been abused;
She's been burned, dishonored, denied and refused.
And the government for which she stands
Is scandalized throughout the land.
She's getting threadbare and she's wearing thin,
But, she's in good shape for the shape she's in.
Because she's been through the fire before,
I believe she can take a whole lot more.
So we raise her up every morning, and we take her down every
night.
We don't let her touch the ground, and we fold her up right.
On second thought, I do like to brag
Because I'm mighty proud of that ragged old flag."
Written by: John R, Cash

OLD GLORY

• Family

While playing baseball in Bryson City, N.C., Claude Crisp Sr., had struck out 26 batters and caught a pop fly on the 27th man, winning the game. That feat won him the distinction of being in "Ripley's Believe It or Not," Bethel Crisp said proudly.

But Claude Crisp Sr. soon learned that he needed more money than what he could earn in baseball, so he went to work in the coal mines. He would alternate days working at Glamorgan Coal Co. and playing baseball in the area, Bethel Crisp said.

The children remember their father playing baseball, making music and telling stories of early attempts by the United Mine Workers of America to organize.

But as time passes, memories fade and they wanted to go and see for themselves the places they left as children and young adults.

They gathered in Norton April 2-4, with a flood of excited chatter hugs and tears, young and old together — Bethel Crisp and his wife Olivia, from Sevierville, Tenn.; their son James Crisp; Wilma Crisp Owens and her husband Joe from Laurel, Md.; Bobby Ray Crisp and his wife Amy, from Murphy, N.C.; Claude Crisp, Jr., from Jonesboro, Ga.; Juanita Crisp Kilpatrick and her husband Robert, from Andrews, N.C. with their two daughters, their husbands and a granddaughter.

Piling into their cars they set out to find their childhood places, where the stories that had been passed down originated.

Along Esserville Road at the Rock Switch intersection, stands a series of trailers, but Bethel Crisp remembers it differently. On that site stood the house where the family lived from 1936 to 1937. Wilma Crisp Owens was born in that house, he said, while

COALFIELD PROGRESS PHOTO/ RON SKEBER

When he wasn't playing semi-pro baseball or working in the coal mines, Claude E. Crisp Sr., loved to play music with his family and friends. He is shown here in the 1930s with a banjo, one of his favorite musical instruments. "He could really make a banjer talk," son Ray Crisp, said of his father's musical talents.

was born in that house, he said, while slowing the car to look, but nothing he remembers still stands.

They travelled farther and found part of the stone building that was the Gardner School, where Bethel Crisp attended school from fourth to seventh grade.

Farther along the road sits Gibson Store, as it has since 1909, Bethel and his brother Ray said they remember being sent to the store for staples like flour and coffee. They said they didn't like to come because it was a long walk from their house and a closer store, which no longer stands, was much more convenient. "But sometimes they didn't have the things we needed," Ray Crisp said. "It was quite a walk."

Under sunny skies, the Crisp clan stopped and crossed the dusty road to explore — surprised and pleased that the store they remembered was still there.

From the store they ventured to find the house they had lived in near Birchfield. When they moved to Wise County in 1930, the family lived in Stevens, Bethel Crisp said. They stayed there for about a year, then moved to a house in Birchfield where they lived in 1931 and 1932.

Driving slowly, looking for anything familiar, they proceeded along Birchfield Road looking for the house. Bethel and Ray Crisp talked about their oldest brother, James, who was born in 1924, but was killed in Belgium during World War II. Before joining the Army and leaving Wise County, James went to work in the mines with their father.

James and their father talked about the union and the pressures the company put on the men not to join. "When the union first came in they came to Glamorgan. That was one of the first places," Ray Crisp said. "The company would threaten to shut the mines down. Now they really wouldn't, but they just wanted to hang the thread of employment over them."

But more than the work in the coal mines, the men associate their father with baseball and music. Claude Crisp Sr. always had friends to play music with, they said.

"They didn't play music at church because they would want to dance and you couldn't do that at church," Ray Crisp said. "They come to our house or go to other people's houses and get together and have a good time."

"He could really make a banjer talk," Ray Crisp said proudly, adding that his father didn't really like working in the coal mines. "He didn't like working period," Bethel Crisp joked back, bringing laughter from the others.

The family members believe their father's athletic talent has been passed down through the family. "Well, Claude Jr. followed Dad in baseball in school," Ray Crisp said. "He could really throw a ball; and all the children too. It's inherited, even in the girls. All the children played softball, baseball, basketball, you name it."

As they talked they realized they'd come to the spot where they had lived on Birchfield Road in 1931 and 1932. Flanked by two trailers and an old storage building, they got out to wander, to talk to anyone who might help them.

They walked up a steep hill and began talking with a woman who said she knew about the house they were looking for. Two rooms of it had been moved and added to her home. Stepping inside, they stepped back in time, amazed to see the old fireplace, walls and floors they knew.

While some looked inside, Olivia Crisp reminisced that Claude Sr.'s wife, Alice Ogle Crisp, helped hold the family together through hard times. "She was one hard worker," she said. "She helped the kids, sewed, cooked, helped all her neighbors. She was the backbone of the family and one very fine woman."

From Birchfield, Bethel Crisp had two more places he wanted to find — the house on Dotson Creek where the youngest sibling was born, Claude Jr., in 1942, and the Hubbard Chapel where the family attended church.

When they got near the house on Dotson Creek, Bethel Crisp stopped to ask some men where it was located.

An older man, Jim Strouth, told him the house was no longer standing, but pointed the way to the lot up a steep embankment.

As they talked, Strouth said he knew Claude Crisp Sr. and James. He said they had travelled to work together for Glamorgan Coal Co., many years ago.

The family was astonished. What were the odds of finding this man 50 years after they had left Wise County? They paused to exchange names and tales before testing their stamina up the embankment.

Wooded, rough and steep was the trip to the lot where the Dotson Creek house had stood.

But, the journey was rewarding. Amy Crisp, Ray's wife, found old bed springs, a coffee pot, a wash basin and an old milk jug, all believed to be left behind by the family 50 years before.

Bethel Crisp, showing little enthusiasm for hiking the steep hill, left some of the group behind and went to find the Hubbard Chapel Baptist Church.

Tucked off the road stood the brick chapel he said he planned to attend on Sunday. To the side of the building, he found a creek and the old wooden bridge that had been there in his childhood. He took pictures of it to mark the day.

Growing weary, he rejoined the group and headed back to Norton for some rest.

Some were amazed at how many links to the past they had found in their weekend trip. But Amy Crisp believes someone else was at work to make the trip so successful.

"I thank the Lord," she said. "It's just the power of the Holy Spirit that's brought us back here and made this possible."

Memories of Bethel Chandler Crisp

Bethel was born 11-7-1925 to Alice and Claude Crisp of East Laport, North Carolina and lived in North Carolina until age 5. Moved to Virginia, raised as a coal miner's son. At age 18 he joined the U.S. Navy. He lost his brother James in Belgium during World War II. When World War II ended, he came home to North Carolina. He later came to Tennessee, worked at Alcoa Aluminum Company, met and married Olivia Helton 10-9-1947, lived in Sevier County, Tennessee.

Had three sons: James William, Howard Donald and Joe Ernest. Retired from Rohm & Haas Chemical Company, Knoxville, Tennessee.

Pastored Churches 40 years.Three Grandchildren: Jennifer Louise, Justin Ernest and Olivia Jean. Two great grandsons: Deven Caleb and Amos Andrew. One great, great grandson: Zachary Christioner.

He was loyal to his Church, his family and his country. He loved sports: Golf, baseball, swimming, hunting, fishing, checkers, traveling land, sea and air. Also loved riding motorcycle, 4 wheeler, horses and roller skates.

Favorite food: Shrimp, cornbread, biscuits & gravy, scrambled eggs, creamed potatoes, ice cream, lemon pie and Juanita's candy. Favorites drinks: Milk and Coke.

His interest's: Church, family and country. Loved pastoring Churches, visiting friends and relatives. Lifes main interest, pointing others to Christ.

What a man! No wonder I loved him!

I wondered again to my old cabin door
And I called for the loved ones I wanted to see.
As I waited the voice that would bid me come in
But nobody answered me.

I called and I called but nobody answered
I searched everywhere but no one could I see
Then I knocked on the door like I oft had before.
But nobody answered me.

My thoughts all turned back to the long, long ago
To the scene of my childhood so happy and free.
Like the Prodigal Son, I wondered back home
But nobody answered me.

I looked here and there, I looked everywhere
I called "oh mother" where can you be?
I called and I called, but alas they had gone
And nobody answered me.

Then I turned away from that dear little home
No more I thought perhaps would I see
But as I turned to go, I called them once more
But nobody answered.

The Mythical Preacher's Wife

Daily works from morn till
night,
Perfect children act just
right,
House is always neat and
clean,
Company may soon be
seen,
Cheerfully at every
meeting,
Smiling nicely with her
greeting,
Slim, trim and always fit,
Confident and quick with
wit,
Thrifty, smart and pretty,
too,
Knows the Bible through
and through,
Cooks and entertains with
zest,
Never worried, never
stressed,
Talent, charm and
patience, too,
Nothing that she cannot
do,
Never existing in real life-
She's the mythical
preacher's wife.

Growing Up In Goose Gap Depression Years

Back in the 1800s when my dad was two years old, the White Caps killed his dad, leaving his mother with seven children. Years later when my dad was nineteen he met and married my mom who was fourteen. They had eleven children, six boys and five girls.

My favorite uncle and aunt lived next door. They had one girl and ten boys. I was born in 1929 depression years. I was blessed by having good parents who had managed to have their own home and enough land to raise enough food to feed a family of thirteen three meals a day. Things didn't come easy. We learned to work young. By the time we could carry a hoe, we was out in the field bursting clods or cutting down weeds. We were never bored. As we grew older, work just came natural.

One of my best friends lived with her mother and one sister and two brothers in our community in a one room house with a dirt floor. Her father was alive but he would not help them. They was at the mercies of their neighbors and the Mountain View Baptist Church. My mom and dad kept three milk cows to furnish milk and butter and sometimes cottage cheese. Dad had horses and mules to till the ground or pull the wagon and sled or they could ride them to various places. Dad also hauled tan bark into Knoxville to sell.

Dad always took good care of his horses. He fed them two meals a day and watered them. He never put them up without curing them down, kept good shoes on them and a clean stable. Sometimes they was out in the pasture field where there was a stream of water.

On the farm we raised enough corn to last through the year, meal for cornbread, plus to feed the horses, cows and chickens. Mom would sometimes make hominy. She made it in the wash kettle, for thirteen it took a big pot. We always had a cane patch in the fall. My dad ground the cane and made molasses. He had a molasses pan and other tools to make molasses (the only one in the community). Our neighbors brought their cane and came to our place to have it made into molasses…"An interesting time."

From the molasses and popcorn we raised, mom made us popcorn balls. My mom also raised enough broom corn to make three or four brooms each year. My dad put up enough hay to winter the horses and cattle (feed through winter). Back then there were no hay balers so he filled the barn with loose hay. Then with the post hole diggers he dug a deep hole and put a long pole in the ground. He knew how to stack the hay around the pole to make it shed water. He always used that first.

My dad had a wheat field where he raised enough wheat so we could have bisquits, gravy, pie crust and cakes the year round. I remember, I liked to help him in the wheat field when he sowed the wheat. First, along the top of the field he drove five foot wooden sticks about every twenty feet apart all the way across. Then he would take the wheat sower full of seed and start sowing. I would come behind him with a hammer and take the wooden sticks
down the hill about five steps and drive them in the ground and on and on until we finished. When time came to cut the wheat, dad cradled it one big arm full after the other then tied it in bundles and shock it (stand the bundles up

right) and later, gather it in the barn before the rain came. In the fall, the wheat threshers came to thresh the wheat. That was an exciting time. The threshers had to spend the night, they had no way to travel to their homes. The straw was blown into a wooden rack my dad had built. The straw would not be wasted, it was used for numerous things. We use it to fill bed tucks (we had no mattresses), ever so often we changed the straw. The first mattress we ever had was a county project. We were judged on how large our family was as to whether we got a mattress or two. A man named John Rambo was over the project. They brought material and set up saw horses and made them in Bluff Mountain School yard.

Dad tried to keep ten or twelve bee hives which furnished honey all of the year. Plus, he made bees wax to use for various things. During all this we had to take care and save enough seeds to plant the next year.

Back to the straw. Under the floor of our house, dad and the boys dug a big low place called a cellar. Every year in the fall we cleaned it out and lined it with new straw and stored potatoes, cabbage, turnips, pumpkins, squash and apples, then covered them over with straw. We also use the straw to bed down the horse stables and dog beds. Dad kept two or three hunting dogs. They were valuable. Dad took them into the mountains, killed rabbits, squirrels and sometimes turkeys which we used for food. He also killed opossums, coons, groundhogs, foxes and other things for hides. He had hide boards where he stretched them inside out and tanned them. Once a year he took them into Sevierville and sold them. The money, it was like the tobacco money...it came in handy.

We kids were never bored. My dad played the banjo. We all liked music. We sang at home, at Church, in school, anywhere! When we were babies, my mom sang and rocked us to sleep. We made our own toys with a piece of rubber from a worn out tire tube, a piece of cloth and some thread. We could make a ball, we used small stones for jack rocks. With a hogs bladder we could make a basketball. With clay mud we could roll it out and bake it and make a marble. We called them "peagibs." We made baseball bats from oak, hickory or dogwood.

There was no electricity or running water. There were two cisterns in our community (hand dug wells), one at the home of Jim and Etta Whaley, one at Mortar Branch School, where they had school years ago. When they closed the school my dad bought the property and my brother Lynn Allen owns it today.

My brother Reece Died at the nursing home in Sevierville. They told him he was the only one there who had an electric toothbrush. He told them he had come a long way from a willow twig to an electric toothbrush. I told him he had come a long way from a Sears & Roebuck catalog to Charmin toilet paper.

Back to our water supply. At our home we had two fifty gallon wooden barrels that set in the drip of our house. We tried to keep it clean and use it for many things.

"Back to our toys." Dad and the older boys made us kids a see saw and a merry go round. I remember I had on a new dress and I knew better than to get on that merry go round with it on. I fell off and hung my dress and tore it bad. A lesson learned. The first time I went to Sevierville, I walked seven miles there and seven miles back with my favorite aunt Sally. I had picked blackberries and sold them and had enough money to buy material for seven new dresses. Mom had a sewing machine and made most of our clothing except for the boy's overalls and pants.

Saturday was an interesting day at our house. Dad had a shop and was the miller in our community. People brought their corn to be ground into meal. They had little money so dad ground their corn into meal for a percentage of their corn. Dad was also a blacksmith he shod their horses and mended their gears, put new handles in their tools, made plow stocks, single trees, sharpened their saws, he could heat a piece of metal and shape it any way he needed too. He had an iron last, so he put new soles on their shoes. He had wax thread he had made from beeswax, so if their shoes was ripped or torn he could fix that too. He cut hair. Back then, very few people owned clippers.

On Sunday morning, our neighbor Odie McCarter, who could not tie his tie came by for dad to tie his tie so he was all dressed up to go to Church. We had chickens to kill when the preacher came for dinner. Mom never killed or took to the rolling store our pullets or hens, it was the roosters who got sold or cooked. Our pullets and hens was for laying eggs

and hatching out chickens. Mom took eggs and sometimes a rooster to the rolling store once a week to buy salt, sugar, coffee, baking powder, soda, coal oil, matches and a little light weight canned or box of raisins. We raised cotton to make quilts. Mom had cotton cards she used to make cotton bats to put between the quilt top and the lining.

In the winter nights after supper, us girls would shut the door between the kitchen and living room and wash the dishes and sing "practice up for Church." Then we would go in around the fire and pick cotton seeds out of the cotton, until dad wised up and made a cotton gin. Our cats were disciplined. We let them come and go in the house, they never got on the beds, chairs or tables. They were valuable, keeping the rats and mice away. The dogs never came inside even though we had no screens. We only had outside toilets til after I was married. That was at home, school or at Church. "I was always afraid there would be a snake. We never threw away a plank or a rusty nail. Our medicine was mostly 'castor oil,' 'turpentine,' 'vicks salve,' 'salts,' 'coal oil' and 'liniment,' an onion poultice. I was eighteen when I was married and had never been to a doctor. Sometimes the county sent someone out to the schools to give shots for 'whooping cough' or the measles. I had a few of them.

There was little money, we always had a tobacco allotment. The more land you owned the more tobacco you could raise and sell. Dad sold it a little before Christmas. We all got new shoes, 13 pair, a treat for Christmas. Dad bought a crate of oranges, a bushel of apples, two or three coconuts, a box of horehound candy, a box of mint candy, chocolate drops, and a little of the coconut balls, because he knew it was moms favorite. The reason she always got raisins from the rolling store, she knew that was dads favorite for Christmas. Mom always made a dried apple fruit cake, a chocolate and a coconut cake. We never put up a Christmas tree, there was no toys, but dad had bought us each a three pound brown paper bag.

They had put in it a apple, a orange, two or three sticks of candy, some nuts, chocolate and coconut candy. We was as happy as a coon. Sometimes two or three weeks would pass and we would still have some of our candy. The fruit we had to eat or it would spoil. Now and then mom would make all of us a big popcorn ball. My dad smoked tobacco mostly some he had grown, but now and then he would buy a can of Prince Albert, and sometimes he would roll his own cigars with brown sugar, honey and vinegar "smelt good." Dad allowed no alcoholic drinks or bad talk around our house. He always kept a little money in the Sevier County Bank in case any of us kids got sick. In mom and dad's offspring there are ten preachers, six deacons and two trustees. Mom and dad never had luxuries for themselves. They only got their rewards when one of us kids made them proud. We loved each other and stuck together and still do.

I, along with my brothers and sisters salute mom and dad for a job well done.

Preachers:
1. Edward Parton
2. David Montgomery
3. Edward King
4. Chris King
5. Wilford Watson
6. Bethel Crisp
7. Justin Crisp
8. Rod Garrett
9. Bill Helton
10. Danny Manning

Deacons:
1. Bruce King
2. Jack Watson
3. James Crisp
4. Chuck Huskey
5. Lynn Allen Helton
6. Bruce Stinnett.

Trustees:
1. Reece Helton
2. Bruce Stinnett.

My Uncle Johnny

My uncle Johnny Helton (my dad's oldest brother) was seventeen when the White Caps killed his dad. He felt responsible for the rest of the family being the oldest child. He first married Mollie McClure. They had three sons: Odas, Hobert and Boyd. Mollie died while the children were young. Later Uncle Johnny married Laura McGill and they had a son, Ernest. When their second son was born Laura and the child both died. Back then, there was few doctors and women only had a granny woman to help them in childbirth. His third wife, Martha England was younger than two of his children. Together, their children were Carl, Alma, Bill, and twins Arthur and Oscar, then Clyde who was killed in World War II, Margie, Lillian, Mary Bell and Elmer. Uncle Johnny had sixteen children. Anyway, through a rough life Uncle Johnny got discouraged, started drinking alcohol.

This is his poem:

> This is what makes me lie, cheat and steal.
> Walk the ridges and miss many a good meal.
> Go down in my pocket and spend my last dime,
> And wear patched overalls in the winter time.

Uncle Johnny had a hard life, but he was our uncle and we loved him. Shortly before he died he told my dad he had got saved. He said I have been saved quite a while and did not tell anyone because I did not know if I could kick the habit of alcohol. But the Lord, he has took away the desire for drinking alcohol.

Uncle Johnny was born 1878, he died 1952. He was 74 years old. He is buried with his wife Martha along with several of their children in the Mountain View Baptist Church cemetery, Sevier County.

My Old Fashioned Mom

She was always so demanding
I remember as a child.
She taught us to be respectful,
While my friends were running wild.
With her rules and regulations,
I was lucky to have a friend!
And when Church began on Sunday,
I was expected to attend.
My mom believed in discipline,
And practiced the golden rule.
She told all my teachers
To make me mind in school.
She was not the modern mother,
I so often hear about,
Where she stood on corporeal punishment,
Never filled my mind with doubt.
I compared my home to prison
Where conditions were the worst.
She'd forbid a casual friendship,
Unless she met them first.
As I grew a little older,
She earned my deep respect.
Not once did we her children,
Ever suffer from neglect.
I'm older now and wiser,
But I think where would I have been,
If I hadn't had her wisdom,
To guide my footsteps way back then.
And I may not be the person

That she wanted me to be,
But I cherish the set of values,
That my mother gave to me.
And I may not often say it,
(Not many children do).
But to all mothers everywhere,
This is just for you!

If I knew it would be the last time
I'd tuck you in more tightly,
And pray your soul to keep.

If I knew it would be the last time
I'd see you walk out the door,
I'd hug you and kiss you-and call you
Back for just one more.

If I knew it would be the last time
We'd spare a minute or two,
I'd stop and say "I love you,"
Instead of assuming you know I do.

If I knew it would be the last time
I'd be there to share your day,
I wouldn't wait until tomorrow,
Letting time with you slip away.

For surely there is a tomorrow
To make up for an oversight,
And we'll always get a second chance
To make everything all right.

There will always be another chance
To say our "I love yous,"
And certainly there's another chance
To say our "What I can dos."

But just in case I might be wrong
I'd like to say I love you,
And hope you never forget.

Tomorrow is not promised to anyone
Young or old alike,
And today might be your last chance
To hold your loved one tight.

So if you're waiting for tomorrow,
Why not do it all today?
For if tomorrow never comes,
You will surely regret the day.

You didn't take the extra time
For a smile or hug or kiss.
And you surely aren't too busy to grant
What may be their last wish.

So hold your loved ones close today,
And whisper in their ear;
Tell them how much you love them,
And that you'll always hold them dear.

Take the time to say "I'm sorry,"
"Forgive me," or It's okay,"
And if tomorrow never comes,
You'll have no regrets about today.

The Flood of 1938
Next photo and newspaper story.
The Ball Family.

An old photo of the funeral of the Ball family, some of the victims of the 1938 flood, is one of the historic pictures published in the 2017 version of Sevier County Memories calendar, now on sale as a fundraiser for Friends of Sevier County Library System.

Remembering the flood of '38

Submitted

In this election season, it's a good time to remember another election day long ago in Sevier County – a day that started well but ended in tragedy for two families and a whole community.

Aug. 4, 1938, Election Day, dawned bright but muggy and hot in Pittman Center. Election Day was a chance for the whole community to socialize. Families walked for miles to reach the polling place, meet and greet their neighbors, vote and return home.

Three days later, the community gathered again, for the funerals of two of those families, tragically lost in a sudden and terrible flood. Not only did eight people drown, but the whole Webb Creek community was left reeling from the devastation.

A photo of the funeral of the Ball family is one of the historic pictures published in the 2017 version of Sevier County Memories calendar, now on sale as a fundraiser for Friends of Sevier County Library System.

Alfred Ball, 37, his wife Lona McCarter Ball, 31, and their four children, aged from 3 months to 11-years-old, lived in a small house in Ball Hollow on Webb Creek, behind the present-day Cobbly Nob. On Aug. 4, 1938, the whole family walked to Fairview polling station to vote. They met Jesse and Eula Whaley Evans, who lived a mile or so up the mountain from the Balls, and the two families walked homeward together.

It started to rain, and the Evanses agreed to wait out the storm at the Ball home. The rain fell in torrents. Estimates vary, but at least 11 inches of rain fell in 24 hours. The water dammed behind fallen trees and collected in underground chambers until the ground crumbled. Around midnight a huge wall of water, mud and debris at least eight feet tall came crashing down Webb Creek, smashing into the Ball house and sweeping it and its eight occupants away.

Their bodies were recovered in the next couple of days, some of them miles away. Pittman Center Mayor Glenn Cardwell was a young boy at the time. He described the flood as "a very devastating and shocking event in my life."

The community gathered to say goodbye to the two families, whose caskets were covered with masses of flowers. Ball family members were buried side by side in the Clear Springs cemetery and the Evans family in the nearby Shults-Whaley cemetery.

Two ironies made the deaths even more poignant: the Balls had planned to move the next week; the flood left the Evanses' house intact.

Many other Webb Creek residents barely escaped the floodwaters that night by jumping out of windows and off their porches. "The whole Webb Creek valley was devastated,"

Please see **FLOOD** | B2

CONTINUED FROM B1

Cardwell remembers. About eight homes as well as barns, corn cribs, livestock, farm machinery, roads, a church, an ambulance, a school bus, a store, bridges, a power plant flume and crops were washed away.

The funeral director from Sevierville had to reach Pittman Center via Newport because Sevier County roads were impassable. According to "Tennessee Tragedies" by Allen Coggins, so many crops were lost that people feared starvation. The blacksmith lost not only his smithy to the floodwaters but also the hog that was going to provide meat for his family that winter, Cardwell

recalled.

Subsistence farming had been the community's main occupation. "If you lost a milk cow, that was bad," Cardwell said. But Pittman Center folks rallied round to help the worst hit families, some of whom were homeless.

The flood "had a ripple effect far and wide," Cardwell said. Area roads remained in bad shape until the late 1940s.

School could not be held for a while. One schoolteacher complained she had to cross Webb Creek 21 times to reach the school. However, the Civilian Conservation Corps, which at that time was building roads and bridges in the Great Smoky Mountains National Park,

"helped revitalize the communities," Cardwell remembered.

Webb Creek was not finished with Pittman Center.

Flooding continued over the decades, though not as destructive as in 1938. In the 1980s teachers had to carry young students out of Pittman Center Elementary School as floodwaters surged in. In 1989, the creek overflowed its banks twice in a month.

So it was a great relief to Pittman Center officials and residents some years later when the Sevier County Board of Education purchased 38 acres on higher ground on which to build the new elementary school.

The 1938 tragedy kept

local residents wary of Webb Creek's powers. "As a child, I felt like I was sleeping behind Niagara Falls," Cardwell said. He wasn't fearful, but he was aware that a flood could happen at any time.

Smoky Mountain Memories calendars containing the photo of the Balls' funeral and other historic local pictures are now on sale for $10 at Seymour and Kodak libraries, at King Family Library in Sevierville, and at some businesses.

Stocks are limited. Proceeds benefit the three libraries.

For more information, call Diane Johnson, Friends calendar committee chair, at 865-235-9733.

I'm glad to say two of my brothers worked for the C.C.C.E. Eliga Andrew Helton and Mack David Helton. It was a great relief to Pitman Center when the Sevier County Board of Education purchased thirty eight acres of higher ground to build a new elementary school.

The Things Around Us

We are pleased with things in and around our home. If we had to choose where we would live, we would choose Tennessee, right here in Sevierville surrounded by Pigeon Forge, Gatlinburg, Knoxville, Seymour, Maryville and the Great Smoky Mountains. Also, my family, our three sons James, Howard and Joe, their wives and children, grandchildren. My brothers and sisters, their families, numerous relatives and lifelong friends.

Our Church is in walking distance "Mountain View Missionary Baptist Church" which was organized when I was four years old. The cemetery where most of my family is buried is nearby. So what more could I ask for? Only for all our friends and family members to let God come into their hearts!

Three Wise Women:
Ask directions, arrived on time, delivered the baby, brought gifts, cleaned the stable, made a casserole and there was peace on earth.

Hickory Trees. A mountaineers observation:
Our Hickory Trees were valuable trees. They were not to be cut or used for firewood to heat with. My dad could use every inch of it for bulgar wagon wheels, the frames of the

wagon, plus plow stocks, single trees, handles for pitchforks, hoes, shovels, and the bark to bottom chairs and stools and even the small twigs to give us kids a little "hickory tea" (whipping) "ouch!"

There is no end to my story. But there is some things our children and grandchildren need to know about Sevier County. I may not have this in order, but they are facts.

Around 1961 the Rebel Railroad, a theme park as in Pigeon Forge. Later it was called Goldrush Junction, then Silver Dollar City and now Dollywood. The train was there from the beginning, 1961.

Tourist began swarming to Sevier County because of its beauty, cool climate and the Great Smoky Mountains. In 1960 Fort Wear came to Pigeon Forge as a petting zoo. Smoky Mountain Car Museum, the Sky Lift in Gatlinburg, Christus Biblical Gardens, the outdoor drama Hunter Hills Theatre, a train ride from Knoxville and through Sevierville for fifty two years.

In 1936 President Franklin D. Roosevelt came to the great Smoky Mountains and again in 1940 to dedicate the Great Smokies, not then a national park. Schools let out so the children and people from far and near could come to get a glimpse of him. My mother, two sisters Nellie and Juanita was in town and saw this. The Great Smoky Mountains National Park was the people's gift to the nation.

President Calvin Coolidge visited and hiked to Mount LeConte. Clarence Darrow and Henry Ford also visited. John D. Rockefeller Jr. gave $5,000,000 if there were matching funds for the amount. Many people pitched in and finally raised the money.

There was over 6,000 landowners to negotiate with to sell and vacate their property in North Carolina, on the other hand, Tennessee permitted a few owners to sell the land and retain a "lifer lease." (Live on the property until their death) the land going to the park upon their death.

You can read about the Walker sisters when land was condemned. They owned 122.8 acres and received $4,750 for it. The sisters lived there together. Their names was Hattie, Martha, margaret, Louise, Polly and Caroline. The only one who ever married was Caroline. She married Jim Shelton. They had seven children: Margaret Leona, Mary Effie, Martha Hazel, John Andrew, Charles, Edith and Stella.

The Walker sisters lived in Little Greenbrier. Louise Susan was the last survivor, she died in 1964. They are all buried in Maddocks cemetery in Wears Valley. The last person to leave the park was Lem Ownby. He died in 1984. He was 94. Today, the Great Smoky Mountains National Park is the most visited in the U.S.A.

The first fire department of Sevierville was just a truck parked behind Temple Milling Company. Later they built a building behind the First Baptist Church. The siren was on a power pole on Bruce Street and later placed on the Court House tower.

The first theatre was the Pines Theatre. Located near Rawlings Funeral Home. A short time later, the Park Theatre was located on Court Avenue near where Dolly's statue now is. The price per ticket was twenty five cents. The first hotel was New Central Hotel 1924.

Some of the oldest businesses in Sevierville:

Whites Grocery Store; Cas Walker Groceries; Raymonds Shoe Store; White Frost Flower Mill; K. Rawlings Furniture Store; The Ten Cent Store; Fines Jewelry; The Corner Store; Dick Allen's Restaurant; Atchley Funeral Home; Rawlings Funeral Home; Post Office; Wade's Department Store; Sevierville Grain and Feed; Cash Hardware; Sevier County Bank; The Bank of Sevierville; Shepherd's Restaurant; Sim's Barber Shop; A.J. King Lumber Company; Mize Lumber Company; Yarberry Hospital; Broady Hospital; Wilson Hospital; The first college was Murphy College.

The first hotel was New Central Hotel which opened in 1924. It set on the corner where the big Sevier County Bank now sets. The Cherokee Textile Mill was the first large employer in Sevier County, located on Middle Creek road and was across from the old Sevier County Hospital. It came from Knoxville and employed about a thousand people.

The first radio station in town was W.S.E.V. It came on the air in April of 1955 as an Am Fm station. One of the oldest newspapers in Sevier County was the Montgomery Vindicator. Some of the oldest doctors were Dr. Gibson; Dr. Ogle; and Dr. Robert Thomas.

In 1976 there was a bicentennial year long celebration, celebrating the United States turning 200 years old. 32 men from Sevier County were killed in World War I,

Chapman Highway was built in 1930 as a two lane paved highway to Highway 411. In 1935 the first Sevier County Fair was held on the Courthouse Lawn. In 1938 two families were drowned in the Smokies when a cloudburst caused so much water to come down Webb's Mountain It killed Alfred Ball, his wife and four children,Jessie Evans, and his wife who were there overnight as guests. They said there were eight caskets in a row.

My brothers Eliga and Mack worked in the C.C.C. Civilian Conservation Corps, one of President Roosevelt's New Deal Programs. There was seventeen camps in and around Sevier County. The men stayed in military style camps or barrick's and trained like they were in the military. Their program employed 4,350 young men. They built hiking trails, horseback riding trails, fire control roads, fire towers and many other things. They received thirty dollars a month with whith twenty five dollars going home to a dependent. The picnic area at the Chimneys was a C.C.C. project.

December 7, 1941 was the surprise attack on Pearl Harbor. Young men from Sevier County went by bus to Fort Oglethorpe, Georgia for their physicals and World War II was on.

My brother Eliga joined the army, he was a medic and fought in the European theatre. During World War II Alcoa (aluminum plant) employed hundreds of men and women from Sevier County. Work buses were provided for transportation. The construction of Douglas Dam across French Broad River took place. Men worked almost around the clock for eighteen months to complete the dam so it could provide hydroelectric power for the war effort.

Most homes back then had a fuse switch box, enough power for lights but not enough for a cook stove. During World War II people bought savings stamps, liberty bonds and a book of rationing stamps necessary to buy many basic items like sugar, coffee, tires, gasoline and shoes. Sugar was converted into gunpowder, torpedo fuel and dynamite. From Sevier County, around one hundred men lost their lives during World War II. Their names are on a bronze plaque in front of the Courthouse at Sevierville.

The stores in Sevier County started closing on Wednesday afternoon and continued that for about sixty years.

March 6 1963 A flood of 14.7 foot flooded Sevierville. Six days later another flood of 16.7 foot. The T.V.A. came up with a plan to alleviate flooding downtown. But before they could, another huge flood came in 1965 of 19.1 foot. T.V.A. had problems with the "Indian burial grounds" families (U.T. McClung Museum). T.V.A. eventually widened the channel of the river and relocated almost a mile of the west prong of Little Pigeon River. T.V.A. straightened the west prong to meet the east prong downstream away from town. Sevierville suffered another flood in February 1966 causing one million dollars in damage. T.V.A. finished the project in 1967 after being delayed by the burial grounds. There was another flood later but not as severe.

Sevier county lost fifteen men in the Korean War trying to stop the spread of communism. In the Vietnam War, my nephew David Helton was damaged by chemicals, "agent orange." He died a few years later.

In the Desert Storm War, my great nephew Max King and many more from Sevier County were severely damaged.

Years ago, Leroy Helton taught agriculture science at Sevier County High School to F.F.A. boys, Future Farmers of America. In 1982 The World's Fair came to Knoxville with exhibits from twenty two countries.

On January 21, 1985, Sevier County had a record low temperature of -24 degrees. In 2008 Gary Wade was elected as the first Sevier County native to sit on the Tennessee Supreme Court. Porpoise Island had a hula

show, supported by people from Hawaii to come to Pigeon Forge around 1985. That was the first job my granddaughter Jennifer Crisp ever had. People liked to go there to hear their music and watch them dance.
There is no end to my story.

The photo on the next page is of Dr. L.C. Benson. Dr. Benson delivered all three of my sons.

He served his community well Dr Benson Delivered All 3 of My Sons

Dr. L. C. Benson retires from active practice

A vital influence in Gatlinburg, of importance to the times and lives of many people in the city and surrounding hills, disappeared when Dr. Leo C. Benson retired.

The ties of the needed and the needing are always strong, and, in the practice of medicine, who is to say who is the needed; which, the needing?

"You don't know what it is like to give up all those years, all my patients," Dr. Benson remarked quietly. "I wish I could go to the office for at least a few hours a day, but I never know what hours will be the ones when I feel up to it."

His eyes brightened. "I try to plug along. I do play some golf," he said. "They give me a few little extra privileges. They let me drive the golf cart on the fairways - and even on the greens." He grinned slyly.

Without his making a point of it, talking with Dr. Benson shows that the practice of medicine is a poor school for retirement. "Taking care of maternity cases and emergencies doesn't go together with fishing and golfing. You are out of reach of the telephone," Dr. Benson said, "so I did a lot of woodworking where I could be close to the phone."

It was 28 years ago that he and his wife, Dorothy, "discovered" Gatlinburg and the Great Smokies. Like most all the other outlanders here, they "just happened to be passing through" and "fell in love with it"; went home, sold out and moved here.

"We didn't know how much of a living we would make, but we did know we could have full lives and be happy," Dr. Benson said.

Here he still echoed the feeling of everyone who ever had to leave home to be in the real home of this mountain land.

But there the outlander steps out and the mountain man speaks:

"I was the only doctor in Gatlinburg - the only one who had been here for some time. And then the word got around that a doctor was in town, from then right on there wasn't any let-up," Dr. Benson said.

He recalls, "There was some kind of a strike up north and none of my equipment had come. All I had was my pill bag. And for some time to come, all I had was my pill bag - but we made out all right."

Before Leo and Dorothy Benson came here, the doctor had a well-established maternity hospital in Fowler, Michigan. They found Gatlinburg in January of 1942 through doctor friends in Greenback, Tennessee, who brought them to see the Great Smokies.

By March of 1942 they were back in Gatlinburg to stay.

When the equipment finally did arrive, Dr. Benson opened an office over Rawling's Cleaners, now Rawling's Motel.

DR. L. C. BENSON and the mountains "we just happened to be passing through" and "fell in love with."

There was a lot of baby borning and sick folks to tend in the city and out in the mountains. In the country, where he could drive, he made calls in a jeep. Where he couldn't, he walked.

And Dorothy went along - either way - to assist. "Doc, we sure are proud you brought your own woman," many an old-timer told him.

Dr. Benson says that his toughest case was delivering twin sons to Mr. and Mrs. Archie Nelson Ogle. The twins weighed a total of 20 pounds at birth.

These were the second set of twins he delivered in that family. "For the first ones I walked in from the highway - and that was quite a walk," he said. Archie Nelson was a farmer in Huskey's Grove.

After three years alone in the practice of medicine here, company arrived, Dr. Ralph Shilling came in to stay in 1945.

"He certainly was welcome," Dr. Benson said.

In 1956 he moved into his new offices on Airport Road. There he practiced until poor health brought on his retirement in March.

The Bensons have two sons, Benny and Craig.

OLIVIA CRISP
2130 Goose Gap Rd.
Sevierville, Tenn. 37876
Ph. 428-1353

The Joys of the Journey
(Chapter 1)

In 1929 (depression years), I was blessed by being born to parents who were farmers. Money & food were scarce. We all worked hard, raising vegetables, corn, & wheat. We had fruit trees: apples, pears, peaches, & plums. We had grape vines, persimmon trees, walnut trees, cows, pigs, chickens, & beehives. We raised tobacco & also had blackberry briars growing in the pasture fields, where we could pick them to sell. We raised tomatoes for the cannery. (My uncle raised beans. He paid us ten cents per bushel to pick the beans! I never have been so tired.)

My Dad would go back in the Bluff Mountain & pick huckleberries, gooseberries, & muskadimes. There were rattlesnakes & copperheads back there so he would never let us kids go. My Dad was a hunter. In the winter, he would kill rabbits & squirrels for food. If he was lucky, he would come back from a hunt near Thanksgiving with a big turkey. He would also hunt & trap other animals. He would stretch their hides on a board or up on the barn wall. Then one day, he would take them into town to sell.

We had no electricity, no running water, but we were blessed with a spring that furnished plenty of water. There we kept a spring box that held our milk, butter, & other things that could spoil in. There were three Poplar tress that shaded the spring & the big iron wash pot, where my mother cleaned things…including us kids.

There was no church building in our community, but there was an empty dwelling house where we had church. A little later, Bluff Mountain School was built so we had church services there. People in the community worked, planned, & prayed together & in 1933 build and organize Mountain View Missionary Baptist Church. Preacher Wiley Garner & Preacher Ezra Adams helped a lot.

We worked hard & we played hard. We made most of our toys, like marbles. We called the types of marbles we made pejibs. We made balls, slingshots, pop guns, bulgar wagons, Merry-Go-Rounds, & see-saws. I had a doll made out of a board. My Dad raised wheat, so we had a straw stack where we had a slide and a tunnel. We also used the straw for our straw-tick beds & we used it for bedding down potatoes, apples, cabbage, & turnips. We had a grape vine swing. We played Annie-Over, Kick the Can, Hoopie Hide, "I Spy", Fox & Dog, Tug of War, Sack Race, Egg Race, Jack Rock, Jump Rope, Mumble Pag, & on and on.

Back to the Church, they used to have revival services morning & night. For the day services, the teachers at the school would march all the children out to the church. I was 12 when my teacher, Rev. Walter Ogle, took us to the revival services. My mother & my sister-in-law & most of the women of the community were there. That was the day I got saved. That night when my dad & the other children came in from the fields, there were tears of gladness. My mother & dad never spoke of love. They showed it in their actions, never thinking of themselves. They were always working hard raising eleven children.

I joined Mountain View Church & spent most of my young life there, except for two years that I lived with my older sister, Zora. Her husband had died & left 2 children. (3 & 5 year old) At that time, I attended Henderson's Chapel Baptist Church. I was blessed by going there to help her. She taught me many things that helped me through life.

We lived in a holler near a river. I learned to swim in that river. We crossed it on a swinging bridge. A branch (water) ran through the yard. We used it for many things. It was clean water, fed by springs further up the mountain. We were blessed with a good garden spot. We used the branch to wash potatoes, carrots, onions, & many other things. We canned a lot of food. She had a good milk cow & lots of chickens. She trapped a eagle which had been killing her chickens. (And then beat it to death)

We had no electricity. We used wood for fuel. We were blessed to have trees near the house. We would take a cross-cut saw & cut down a tree. We would saw a few blocks & she would split it while I rested. She always shielded me. She taught me to clean house, cook, sew, & crochet…only I couldn't tell what it was when I was finished crocheting! No one lived in sight. We always kept a loaded gun. There were a few times we were thankful for a loaded gun. Sometimes we had to pull it out. During this time I rode a bicycle to school, 5 miles morning & evening. She was finally able to build a new house on the other side of the river. She was twenty-seven when her husband died, & she never re-married. Her son became a Baptist preacher & her daughter a nurse with a Bachelor's Degree.

I came back to Goose Gap & soon met and married Bethel. He was just out of the Navy & worked at Alcoa. He just "happened" to see me walking to church one morning. Soon after we married, James William & Howard Donald were born. They were small when we moved to Detroit, Michigan to get **rich**! Bethel worked 2 jobs, no church. There was a church down the street, but it was not Baptist. Alcohol was everywhere. The Lord was there. I prayed more. I could feel him all around me.

We came back to Tennessee & a third son, Joe Ernest, was born. Soon after, Bethel started to go to church with us & got saved. He soon got the call to preach. Walden's Creek Baptist Church called him to be their pastor. I was concerned whether or not I could be a worthy preacher's wife. I prayed a lot, but again, God had some good people there who made me feel loved & needed. As we went to other churches, God always filled our needs. We met many people who became our life-long friends.

Rose Houk

You have probably read about the Walker Sisters who owned 122.8 acres of land in the Great Smoky Mountains.

For their land they received $4,750. The sisters lived together. Their names were Hatti, Martha, Margaret, Louise, Polly and Caroline. The only one who ever married was Caroline. She married Jim Shelton and had seven children I have previously listed.

When my husband, Reverend Bethel C. Crisp was the pastor of Valley View Missionary Baptist Church in Wears Valley, a Church that was first built in the Smoky Mountains, in Elkmont near where the Walker Sisters lived, but had been taken down and moved to Wears Valley, Effie lived in the upper end of the valley. Rosie Husky and I took the G.A.s up to her home to share Scripture and songs. While there, news came that the war, Desert Storm had broke out. It caused great sorrow. My great nephew, Max King was over there. He was damaged badly. He lived to come home but he died a few years later. He is buried in the veterans cemetery.

Before we left, Effie gave me a poem she had wrote and a picture of the cabin where her mother was born. I'm enclosing a poem she wrote about The Walker Sisters Cabin on the 5th Sunday in October 1966.

"My Mother's Homeplace."

1.   I wandered back again today
        To the old log cabin once more
There was no "visitors welcome" sign
        Hanging outside the door.
        2. Though tacked upon the door,
    "Now closed" a printed sign read,
    "Property of the U.S. Government,
        No trespassing" it said.
        3. There was no friendly hello
        No welcome smile so sweet
        Bidding me to come inside
        And rest my weary feet.
        4. Only silence greeted me
        No gaity or laughter,
    Only the chirp of a Katydid
        Perched upon a rafter.
    5. The old corm crib that once was full
        Stands empty there today.
The old stock barn and dry house too
        Have both been torn away.
6. The spring where once we quenched our thirst
        On a hot summer day,
The path was overrunned with weeds
        No flowers bloomed by the way.
7. No blue smoke from the chimney curled,
        Everywhere cobwebs clung.
Upon the door that once stood open,
        A large padlock was hung.
    8. No bonnets hung on the wooden peg
        In the logs of the kitchen wall,
    No aroma from the kitchen came,
        No welcome mealtime call.

9. I walked around to the garden gate,
Where once was planted seeds,
The gate upon its hinges sagged,
The plot was overgrown with weeds.
10. I bowed my head in silence there,
My eyes were filled with tears.
Could this be the same old house
Where I had come for years?
11. The windows they were boarded up,
I couldn't see inside,
I longed so much to open the door
And view the old hearthside.
12. Where once the family gathered around,
So snug by the fireside warm?
The hands that tilled the fertile soil,
Of this old rocky farm?
13. Their bodies lie in deep repose
Upon a windswept hill,
Where whispers sweep at evening tide
And the whippoorwills call so shrill.
14. They are resting there in peaceful sleep,
Undisturbed by mortal sound,
Waiting the resurrection day
when Gabriel's trumpet shall sound.
15. Then they'll move to a cabin on high,
And be happy forever more,
Where no doors will be closed
Or padlocks hung
On heaven's golden shore.

Written by Effie Phipps
After a trip to the Walker Sisters Cabin

Mary Had A Little Boy

Mary had a little boy, whose soul seemed white as snow.
He never went to Sunday School because Mary wouldn't go.
He never heard the stories of Christ that thrilled the childish mind.
While other children went to church, this child was left behind.
And as he grew from babe to youth, She saw to her dismay,
The soul that seemed snowy white had turned a dingy gray.
Realizing he was lost, she tried to win him back.
But now the soul that once seemed white, has turned a dingy black.
She even started back to church to Sunday School, too.
She also begged the Minister, Is there something you can do?
The Minister tried but failed. And said, "We're way too far behind."
I tried to tell you years ago, but you would pay no mind.
And so another soul is lost that once seemed white as snow.
The Sunday School could have helped but Mary wouldn't go.

Memorys Of Home . A Saturday For Instance.

All us kids rolled out early, we could smell biscuits & gravy,we
knew there would be milk to drink and a little butter,black berry
jam and maybe some apple butter.
Dad had already gone to the barn to feed the stock, for this was
going to be a busy day at the shop. People would be coming early
to get corn ground horses shod tools sharpened new handles put in
maddochs,& Axes, harnesses to mend some would need their hair
cut, gears repaired others would just want to visit & catch up on
the news.
Mom fixed the dish water for me to stand in the chair and wash
the dishes while she went to milk the cow's. When she was out of
sight I quickly got down , because I wanted to take a peek in
the meat room, which was a little scary" a room without
any window's, where Ham & Side meat hung from the
ceiling, there was canned goods, crackling's a string of hot
pepper, lye soap and other things, I wanted to climb the
ladder that went up stairs and look around.
I saw Grannys old side saddle some cob webs a few bottles
of wine (put up there to age), I eased back down and went
to the bedroom I saw the quilt pack (where we
foundAnnice) and the wee bed where Reece & Juanita slept
, a loose board in the floor, I saw a window shaped like a
knothole, and old trunk where we kept things that belonged
to Granny and aunt Donnie.
I went back in the living room and saw the fireboard above
the fireplace where the old 8 day clock struck every
hour.Dads tobacco can , A box of matches,a rifle hung over
the door, a shotgun over the bed, I went back into the
kitchen where pots and pans hung on the wall, a razor strap
hung there used to sharpen Dads razor and other things!
and odd shaped window was near the old wood cook

stove, a cat ran out the cat hole ,a towel hung on a nail
above the washbole, a long table with a bench at the back a
fly paper ribbon hung overhead, the old square churn sat
full on the floor, we kept our piano in the kitchen only a
few people knew we had one I was still playing it when
Mom come back from milking.
She said child take this milk & put it in the spring box &
bring back a bucket of water, every one had chores to do so
the beds were soon made the house dusted & swept, Sat.
was a day the yard had to be swept too,my sister Zora was
the keeper of the flowers in the summer there was holly
hawks larkspurs dahilas old maids Easter lilies not to
mention the lilac in the front yard, a big oak tree with a tire
swing, stood near the porch steps,(just enough room for
Dad to drive the horse and wagon through,) four or five
beehives sat on the other side,(where Zora jumped off).
I stopped to swing awhile, and smell the lilac blooms, I
walked up five porch steps, set in a straight backed chair,
my wooden doll lay on the handrail, a broken mirrow was
tacked upon the porch post, underneath on a nail hung the
wash pan Dad used for shaving, the structure was weather
beaten, reminded me of Ody Mc Carters Sunday morning
visit to get his tie tyed.
I wantedto go up to the barn and look around, I saw a Big
straw stack where the threshers had been.I peeked in at
Mert & Tex they were still eating corn, I went to the apple
orchard and ate a few green apples, I checked the blue birds
nest out in the old fence post, I walked around the hill to
see if I could see Aunt Sally and uncle George, I met Joe
Rudd,(He had a little rusty knife in his hand) on my way
back I stopped at the out house where I was always afraid

there would be a snake. I helped Mom run a chicken down,
she was going to wring its neck to have for Sunday
dinner,for come Sunday we were sure to have company.
I went down to the shop to take Dad a fresh bucket of
water, the men were gathered in. it was a busy and exciting
time.(sometimes things got broken,And the wrong person
got blamed).
I looked around Dad had the corn mill running,(did you
ever smell fresh ground meal?) He had the bellows blowing
and was working with a piece of red hot iron, I noticed the
old molasses pan, and wheat cradle hanging high and dry.
I went outside under the apple tree and ate another apple,
the peaches were still too green.I looked in the grape
vineyard to see if the grapes were getting ripe, I noticed a
wooden barrell sitting in a corner of the corn crib,(Juanita
was leaning against the wall) She looked sick.
The day was passing fast, Mom was busy trying to prepare
for Sunday, cooking some cakes or pies, carrying up
enough water to fill a wash tub to give all us little ones a
bath and head wash.
Dad & Mom worked hard, always thinking of us, never
taking time for themselves. They never spoke of love, but
they showed it, raising eleven children.
NO BLACKSHEEP, NO DUDS,
MOM AND DAD . We salute you for a job well done!!!

Organization Of Mountain View Church
October 8, 1933

The council to organize the Church was begun by electing E.E. Adams Moderator
And J.E. Price as Clerk. Then the council proceeded to business first by enrolling
names of Deacons in council, second by enrolling all Ministers, and then by reading
letters, which was done and adopted. Then the council named the Church .
(Mountain View Baptist), which was adopted.
Then the Church covenant was read to the Church and adopted by members of the
Church. The Church elected E.E. Adams as Clerk and Treasurer, then the following
brothers were elected Deacons when - ordained: Arlie Ramsey, Lee Myers, and
W.W. Price. The Council- was given the members' right hand of church fellowship.
 The doors of the Church was opened and the following members recived : Kate
Ogle, Beatrice McGill,Mrs Jessie Price, Johnny Price, and Wilburn Helton,-(when
they submit to baptism).- They adjourned to meet on Saturday night before the
second Sunday in November of 1933, This 8th day of October 1933. E.E. Adams,
Moderator; J. Price, Church Clerk.

Records From The
Original , Moumtain View Baptist Church

 The Mountain View Church decided to build a Church house of Worship and after
receiving a tract of land for the Church, donated by Brother W.W. Price, a building
committee was appointed. This committee consisted of Brother L.S. Sutton, Joe
McGill, and George Helton. They began their duties October 2, 1935 and worked
untiringly until the church was completed. Special honor is due this committee and
especially Brother Sexton who served as chairman and treasurer of the building
Fund. He put forth wholehearted and untiring efforts.

The timber for the lumber was donated by the Church Members and the people of
the community, and we are more than grateful for their Well wishes and wish to
express our thanks to them. A committee for soliciting funds was appointed by the
Pastor. They tried to outdo each other in soliciting, and in all they collected $344.58.
We wish to express our heartfelt thanks to each and all who contributed for this
cause, however large or small, to a most worthy cause.I am sure each will receive a
just reward at the final judgement, when the Lord says you have been faithful in a
few things, enter now into the joys of the Lord.
Another committee was Appointed and designated as an equipment, Committee.
Its purpose was to secure seats and fixtures.

Come, Sing, and Pray

If your load is getting heavy and your journey seems too long,
Come on down to Mt. View, join us in an old time song.
You are sure to get a blessing from the pulpit to the pew,
You will hear some old time preaching and the spirit will renew.

Yes, this church will give you welcome in a humble sort of way,
You can see God's love about them as you enter day by day.
Join our fellowship and service, what is church life all about?
Let the spirit of God guide you as you pray and sing and shout.

Then tell others of the blessings, lead some weary soul to God.
Tell them how we talk of Heaven, share our worries as we trod.
Tell them how our Savior loves them travelling down life's great highway.
Listen, friend, now as I welcome, come and sing and pray.

Come, sing, and pray, come, sing and pray.
And the burden of this life will fade away.
With your friends and family come, and worship God and see.
Oh, I welcome you today, come and sing and pray.

Song written by Una Kate Price Ogle

YOUTH SPEAKS TO PARENTS

In the book, Parents on Trial, by David Wilkerson, 1 suggestions were made by youth to their rents:

1. KEEP YOUR COOL: Kids need the confidence that only a steady hand and a settled soul can offer.

2. DON'T GET HUNG UP on activities that keep you too busy to establish good communications with your children. Father should set aside time for family. Mothers should be at home to supervise their children.

3. DON'T GET STRUNG OUT. Stay away from liquor and pills.

4. BUG US A LITTLE. Use strict but loving discipline. Show us you are wise and strong enough to be boss.

5. DON'T BLOW YOUR CLASS: Keep the dignity of parenthood. Don't try to dress and act like teenagers. Kids need to know their parents are adults.

6. LIGHT US A CANDLE. Show us the way to faith. Be an example of faith at work.

7. TAKE THE WORLD OFF YOUR SHOULDERS. Talk to us about morals, love, life, eternity, peace of mind and values. Let us know we can count on you when things get up tight.

8. SCARE US. When you catch a child in his first encounter with wrong, punish him. Be sure he understands what he has done wrong and why it is wrong. Let him know you are punishing him because you love him and are concerned about him, not because you want to get even.

9. CALL OUR BLUFF. Stand firm and don't let us con you.

10. BE HONEST WITH US. Tell your children the truth. Be generous in praise. When it comes time to criticize your child, he will then believe you and respect your judgment.

A seventeen year old discussed with his father about his need for a car. The father agreed but thought he needed to improve on a few things first: like his school grades, helping around the house and attending Church more regularly and he thought it would be a good idea to get a haircut.

A few months passed and the subject came up again. He said dad I have brought my grades up a little and I'm helping mom around the house and I've been attending church more regularly. His dad said, how about the hair cut? His son said, dad I read in the Bible where Jesus had long hair. The father quickly replied son if you had read on a little further you would find that Jesus walked nearly everywhere he went.

A couple from Minneapolis decided to go to Florida to thaw out during One particularly icy winter. They planned to stay at the very same hotel where they spent their honeymoon 20 years earlier. Because of hectic schedules, it was difficult to coordinate their travel schedules. So, the husband left Minnesota and flew to Florida on Thursday, with his wife flying down the following day.

The husband checked into the hotel. There was a computer in his room, so he decided to send an e-mail to his wife. However, he accidentally left out one letter in her e-mail address, and without realizing his error, he sent the e-mail. Meanwhile.....somewhere in Houston, a widow had just returned home from her husband's funeral. He was a minister of many years who was called home to glory following a sudden heart attack The widow decided to check her e-mail, expecting messages from relatives and friends. After reading the first message, she fainted. The widow's son rushed into the room, found his mother on the floor, and saw the computer screen which read:

>To: My Loving Wife
>Subject: I've Arrived
>Date: 8 Jan 200

I know you're surprised to hear from me. They have computers here now and you are allowed to send e-mails to your loved ones. I've just arrived and have been checked in. I see that everything has been prepared for your arrival tomorrow. Looking forward to seeing you then! Hope your journey is as uneventful as mine was.   PS Sure is hot down here!

My Dad

This is my speach I Made at Mt View Missinary Bapt. Church years ago

William Andrew Helton (Bill) Born March 28-1892.
His Father was Eliga Helton. Born May 16-1857.
His Mother was Ellender Clinton Helton Born July-7- 1860.

Dad had (2) brothers Johnny & George. (4) sisters. Margaret.
Donnie. Mary &Sally. My dad was 2 yrs old when the White
Caps Killed his dad, he said the only thing he could remember
was the church bell ringing.

They say my grand paw was a wealthy man in his day owning
Different parcels of land. Grand Maw had a house keeper to help
with the house work and tending to the children. Grand paw had
sold his land on Waldens Creek road.(the property where
Yesterday/s Antiques sits today), he had planned to take his
family and go out west where his older brother had gone a few
months before. The day he was killed he had closed the deal on
selling his property. But before leaving Sevierville he was
deputized by the sheriff posse to protect a family from a severe
beating by the white caps. It was late in the day and he was
traveling by horseback. There was no time to come home so he
and his comrades started to the victim/s home, over on the battle
hill near Hendersons springs. There they met the White Caps.
The White Cap book says perhaps there was 100 shots fired
several was killed. Grand paw was one of them. When his body
was picked up there was no money in his pockets.

This happened in the year 1894 Grandpa was 31 yrs old.
Grandma was expecting her 8th Child the trauma of his death
caused her to lose the baby. Grandpa was buried in the Shilo
cemetery at Henderson/s chapel Baptist church.

Dads brother Johnny was the oldest child 17 yrs old at the time.
The burden of becoming the man of the family devastated him.
He turned to alcohol, Grandma and 7 children had a hard time
trying to survive on a farm in Goose Gap. She held on to what
was right. I am proud to say my Grandma Ellender Helton, who
I am named after. Her name is the first name on the Mountain
View Missionary Baptist church roll. She lived to be 82 yrs old,
and is buried in Mountain View Baptist Church Cemetery.
When my dad was 19 yrs old he met and married Harretta
Carolyn Ward June 25th 1911 Two days before her 15th
birthday.

Dad grew up in hard times, but he had will power. Shortly
after him and mom married he bought ? acres of land from his
uncle. His uncle told him after he paid the down payment he
could go ahead and build the house then pay the rest later. Dad
did that but when he finished paying for the land his uncle would
not make him a deed for it. So he had to pay for the land again.
He learned a lesson there and he always told us kids never build
on property you don't have a deed far. The house dad built was
where (8) of us (11) children was born, it was a four room house
including the meat room where we kept our meat & canned
goods. Home made lye soap strings of hot pepper & other things
we also kept things in the attic. We had a big long table in the
kitchen with a bench at the back where all the little kids sat.
Mom and dad both sat on the same end of the table near the
coffee pot, my dad liked to drink coffee. He smoked Prince Albert
tobacco, plus he raised his own tobacco and some times rolled his
own cigars using a little brown sugar, vinegar & syrup. He taught
himself many things, his childhood years offered little education.

Dad lived next door to his brother George they always got along
well, helping each other out in their younger years they hauled
tan bark by horse and wagon in to Knoxville. Uncle George had
ten boys and one girl. Dad had six boys and five girls.

I was born 1929 depression years. I remember my dad could do
many things, he never let his family go hungry. He had a good
helpmate mom. Together they raised all kinds of vegetables corn
and wheat. Dad had beehives, pigs, cows, chickens. mules. He set
out all kinds of fruit trees, sometimes he grafted them, he had
grape vines, walnut And permission trees. Dad & Mom taught us
kids well by the time we could carry a hoe we were bursting
clods, cutting weeds in the field. There was no such thing as
sitting around getting bored with nothing to do. We learned to
work when we were young. So as we grew it was just natural to
work. My oldest brother Mack by the time he married Owned 75
acres of land it was all paid for. He cleared a big part of that
with a Maddock and axe. I remember taking him cool water out
in the fields. My Dad had a corn mill, on Saturdays people would
bring corn to be ground into meal, They also brought tools to be
sharpened & repaired. He was a blacksmith. He could take a
piece of metal heat it and shape it into different things like a
shovel, dog irons. He made plow stocks handles for maddocks,
picks, hammers. hoes, and on and on. He would put shoes on
horses and mend their gears. On Saturdays he was also the
neighbors barber, he was a cobbler he had an iron last with
different sizes of feet. He would take beeswax thread and sew the
shoes if they were ripped or he could put leather or rubber soles
on the shoes. He could ring hogs dehorn cattle , Castrate pigs
calves and horses. He always took good care of his horses, he
never failed to curry them down, water them, feed them morning
and night. Dad built our first barn out of logs, we always had a
big hay stack, made by the wheat threshers who come in the fall
to thresh the wheat dad had raised. Us kids played on the straw
stack but we used the straw for a lot of things like like bedding
down potatoes, turnips, cabbage. Straw for the bed ticks, in the
spring we had spring cleaning day. Carrying everything outside
but the cook stove and dining table. Took all the paper off the

walls, scalded the walls, the floor with eagle lye water, scalded the bed and slats so if there was any chinches it would kill them. Then we repapered the walls with news papers and paste made out of flour and boiling water. We washed and dried the straw ticks and filled them up with new straw, we looked forward to sleeping way up high. We always raised enough corn and hay to feed our animals. Dad would take the posthole diggers and dig a hole, put a pole in the ground and stack hay in a way it would shed water. There was no way to bale hay back then the barn would not hold enough loose hay to last through the winter. We used the hay stack first, dad always built his own sleds, he made wagon beds with a seat (with springs) . He even made a cotton gin where we seeded the cotton, Mom used to make quilts. Dad tilled the fields with a turning plow. Used a clod buster harrow and a single foot plow to lay off the rows. Then for working the crops he had a double foot and a three foot plow. He cut hay with a mowing machine pulled by horses, then the hay rake, we used a pitchfork, loading it on the wagon then bringing it to the barn. The wheat dad cradled by hand.

Dad was a good hunter he always used a twenty two rifle as to not shoot up the meat too bad, he taught us kids how to use a gun the safe way. Dad butchered hogs and calves for meat for the family he killed Opossums, ground hogs, coons and foxes stretched their hides on boards or the side of the buildings. Then one day he would take them into town and sell them.(Some one told a tale about their hunting dog, said all they had to do was set a board out, and the dog would go out and bring back a opossum that fit it, till one day the woman left her ironing board out and they never saw the dog again.) They cut down trees with a cross cut saw, as long as I can remember Dad had a big stack of lumber in the old barn, he planned for the new house, for many years. I was around 14yrs old when it was completed. It was one of the nice houses in goose gap. Then we built the new barn I can

remember being on the tip top standing up helping dad, I was as
happy as a coon. Dad built a log chicken house we ordered 50 or
100 baby chicks while the weather was still cold, the chicken
house had a furnace underneath where we used wood to heat it.

Dad never allowed any bad talk or drinking around our house
(even uncle Johnny). Uncle Johnny had a hard life working hard,
and drinking it up. He had (3) wives and (16) children. He finally
kicked the alcohol habit a short time before he died in year 1952
he was 74 yrs old. He is buried in Mt. View Baptist Church
cemetery. He was our blood kin and we loved him. In the !fall
Dad liked to take a week to go hunting, back to the Baker place
on Bluff Mt. With his brother in law Charlie Shular and his
brother Manker. It was back there where Dad got saved. My
Mom and uncle Charlie had been praying for Dad a long time. I
was real young but I can still remember Dad walking up the aisle
of Mt View church and telling everyone he had got saved.

In his later years he liked to go into Sevierville on Saturdays,
and buy things he needed and sit on the bench at the court house
and talk to old friends. We were always interested in what he had
to say that night. He had a lot of jury duty. He always exercised
his right to vote, he was a republican but he would vote for a
Democrat if he thought he was the right man. My Dad played the
banjo, he would let me dance but Mom would not. Most of the
time he dressed in overalls and a long sleeved shirt. On special
occasions he would wear pants, he turned his shirt sleeves under
instead of rolling them up. He wore a grey felt hat he had a good
one for Sundays. And an old one for work days. I cannot
remember seeing him wearing a cap or a short sleeved shirt, and
I never remember seeing him with no shirt on. My Dad was not
perfect, but he always obeyed the Law of the land. He helped his
neighbours raised (11) Children the best he could. He was to
harsh with the older ones, whipping them too hard making them
walk the chalk line. I think he was afraid one of us would turn

out to be an outlaw. So he held on too tight, as years passed he learned too loosen up and let go. You know experience is the best teacher. He learned from his mistakes, as we all do. Dad had cancer and died October –25th-1952, he was 60 yrs old. He is Buried in the Mt. View church cemetery. I can say and I think all my brothers and sisters can say . **I am proud William Andrew Helton is my Dad.**

The Hanging of the Court House

The one who had toiled in the fields, the shop the grinding meal. Shoeing Horses, sharpening tools. Cutting hair, raising 11 Children Teaching us the ways of life

My brother Mack David Helton

Born August 19 1912. Died January 28 1998. Age 85.

Macks first well paying job was the C.C.C. Conservation Corps. The C.C.C. was one of President Roosevelt's "New Deal" programs. At the peak of the C.C.C. program there was seventeen camps either in or around Sevier County. The reason they called them camps, the men employed in the program stayed in military style camps and barracks and trained like they were in the military.

This program employed 4,350 young men who worked mostly in the great Smoky Mountains National Park, building hiking and horseback riding trails, fire towers and many other types of construction work. 'The picnic area at the Chimney's' was a C.C.C. project.

The boys employed at the C.C.C. received Thirty dollars a month with twenty five dollars going home to dependents. As time passed, Mack had a job cutting timber in the mountains of Virginia. While working there he had a accident and his knee cut pretty bad and had to come home to Sevierville, Tennessee. Shortly after that, that company bought the timber on Bluff Mountain in Sevier County, Tennessee and brought their families and saw mill and set up on Bluff Mountain and hired Mack back.

They cut all the trees that was suitable for lumber, then the saw mill moved on. During this time my uncle Oscar Ward, my mother's brother and my aunt Mary, my dad's sister owned seventy five acres of land on Helton Road in Sevier County located on Helton Road off Goose Gap Road.

They failed to pay their land taxes and their property was sold on the steps of the Courthouse in Sevierville.

Mack was unmarried and bought the land and was debt free when he married. During World War II Alcoa, the Aluminum Company of America in Blount County, Tennessee employed hundreds of men and women from Sevier County. A bus owned by Roy Fox, owner of Fox Grocery Store, located on the corner of Goose Gap and Waldens Creek Road transported the workers.

In 1930 Chapman Highway became a paved highway to 411. At age twenty five Mack married Hazel Cutshaw. They had two children, Maxine, who married Bruce Stinnett and Helen, who married Rev. Edward Parton. Mack is the only one in our family of eleven children to be divorced. It really hurt him and he almost lost his mind. He worked and retired at the Aluminum Company of America in Blount County.

Years passed and he met and married Katherine Johnson, a good woman. They bought a home and lived in Maryville until Katherine was disabled and had to go to the Blount County Hospital in Maryville. They had her on life support several days before she died. Most of her family turned against Mack because he didn't have her took off of life support after the Doctor told him there was no way for her to get better.

Mack was in a daze. He knew he was going to have to have some money, he had money in the bank and went by and got several hundred dollars and came back to the hospital. He got out of his car in the parking lot and decided to count his money to be sure he had enough. The wind was blowing and he was so shaky the wind blew that money every way. Mack got so nervous and sick they had to put him in intensive care there at Blount Hospital.

 After Katherine died and was buried Mack sold their home there in Blount County and bought a new brick home just outside Sevierville on Newport Highway next door to Parton's automotive services owned by his daughter Helen and her husband Edward Parton.

 Bethel and I was in Sevierville one day and decided to go up and see Mack and his new home. He was outside when we got there, we went on in and he showed us through his home which was really nice. Everything spick and span, not a thing out of place.

 I noticed he seemed anxious after he sat down. He would jump up and go look out the window and go into the kitchen and take a sip of water. I asked him if he needed to go somewhere, he said no. I said, are you expecting company. He said no. So we didn't stay long.

 Bethel and I got outside and I said I wanted to go up to see Helen who lived real close. So we went up and I asked her about her dad and told her how he was acting. She said I will see about him. So the next day Helen called me and said her doctor there at Sevierville said Mack would have to go to Fort Sanders Hospital in Knoxville. Helen took him there and found out he had lung cancer. A day or two passed and Helen had been with him all the time and was getting tired. She called and asked me if I could come and spend the night while she went home to take care of business, shower and clean up. So Bethel took me down there and a little after midnight I heard a familiar voice of someone walking in the hall. I went and looked out and it was Alma Ward our first cousin and her and Mack was about the same age and had always been close. She was having to walk with the help of a roller walker and a old friend. She had heard that Mack was bad sick and came to see him after twelve o'clock at night. I had her to come up close and I woke him up and asked him if he knew who she was. He looked and said Alma Ward. They talked only a few minutes and he drifted off. I was so thankful she made a big effort to come see him.

Seven weeks after the day the doctor at Sevierville said he had cancer he was in the Mountain View Missionary Baptist Church cemetery with Katherine. Date of death July 6, 1992, age 70.

My sister Mary lZora Helton

 Born October 29, 1914. Died October 14, 1981. Age 66.
Lou Gehrig's disease. Buried in Shiloh Church Cemetery.
My oldest sister Zora born into a family of eleven children.
In depression years she was like a mother as well as a
sister to us younger children. Helping with the housework,
babysitting, cooking and working in the fields; she was the
one who took care of the outside, raking and keeping the
yard swept, planting and taking care of the flower's: we
had flowers blooming from early Spring to late Fall.

She was twenty two when she married Frank
Montgomery. They had two children, David Ellis age five
and Mary Helen age three. Frank had heart problems and
died March 19, 1943. Age 31. I was blessed by going there
to help her. She taught me many things that helped me
through life.

 We lived in a holler near the river on Divide Road. The
river was near by and we had to cross the river on a
swinging bridge every time we went to Church. I soon
learned to swim. There was a branch that run through the
yard. It was clear water which came from springs higher up
on the mountain. We used it for things like washing
potatoes, carrots and onions we got out of the garden. We
also washed muddy shoes and garden tools.

She canned many things from the garden plus
blackberries, made jams and jellies. She also had plenty of
milk, butter and cottage cheese. She raised chickens. She
trapped and killed an eagle that was killing her chickens.
There was no electric, we used wood to cook and heat the
house. We had trees nearby so we took a crosscut saw
and cut down a tree. We cut off a few blocks then she split

them while I rested. She always shielded me. She used the wheelbarrow to bring the wood to the house
While I helped the children over the rough places. She always made whole wheat biscuits for breakfast and gave the kids cod liver oil in a spoon, no capsules. She made the first dress I looked like I was grown up in. It had a sailor collar. No one lived in sight, we always kept a loaded gun. There was times we were thankful for a loaded gun.

During that time I had to finish my school year out so I rode a bicycle back to Bluff Mountain School. It was five miles morning and evening. Zora was finally able to build a house on the other side of the river near Hendersons Chapel Baptist Church.

She was never treated with the respect she truly deserved. Some of the family members wanted to adopt the children but she said no and braced herself up, worked, scraped and raised the children on her own. David became a Baptist minister and Mary Helen a registered nurse. Life was hard but she died with dignity and presence that commands respect, praise and stateliness. Proverbs 31:10 "Who can find a virtuous woman? For her price is far above rubies."

My brother Hugh Wilburn Helton

My brother Hugh Wilburn Helton was born March 16, 1917. Was the first one of mom and dad's kids to get married, even though Mack and Zora was older. Wilburn met and married Dorothy Irene Rule when he was nineteen. They had two children, Iva Irene and Jo Ann. Iva was my mom and dad's first grandchild. I think Wilburn's first paying job was helping build the road across the Great Smoky Mountains. Before the road was built, there was only something like a trail from Gatlinburg Tennessee to Cherokee North Carolina. I have heard that Bethel's grand paw, David Ogle and his first wife lived at the foot of Smoky Mountain on the North Carolina side.

When his wife, Lucy Cole Ogle died leaving him with four children, Elizabeth, Zora, Maude, and Alice "Bethel's mom." They say he brought the children and all their belongings across the Smoky Mountains on a donkey, the way I understood it there was a road mostly like a trail that had been cleared off and three or four small houses or they called them huts where travellers could stay, spend the night and rest where they had access to a spring or water of some sort. So it was really helpful when they got a paved road from Gatlinburg Tennessee to Cherokee North Carolina.

I remember the year when Roosevelt was president and he came through Knoxville, Sevierville, Pigeon Forge and Gatlinburg, being in a convertable, people were lined up all along the road to get a glimpse of the president. My mother and two of my sisters was in Sevierville and got to see that. Roosevelt was on his way to the top of the Great Smoky Mountains to dedicate it. It really is something we are proud of. So, "Don't let the Smokey Mountain smoke get in your eyes, if you do, I'm telling you" you'll never, never want to go away again. "If the Smokey Mountain Smoke gets in your eyes." God has blessed us by letting us live in the foothills of the Great Smoky Mountains. Wilburn always tried to help everyone who needed it. Our sister Zora, who was a widow with two small children got Lou Gehrig's disease and had to be took into Knoxville to the doctor every few days.

No one in the family had a reliable automobile so Wilburn went to Sevierville and bought a new car. He had never drove a car so the dealer took him on a little spin down to the "Y" on Chapman Highway and had him to drive back to Sevierville. Then Wilburn drove the car home and continued to take Zora to her doctor appointments until her death.

The first property Bethel and I owned we bought from Wilburn. It was hard times, we had two sons and was renting a house from my dad. Wilburn sold us four acres at a real bargain and told us to go ahead and build us a house and when we got till we could, we could pay for the land. That's what we done. Wilburn helped us get on our feet, I have been forever grateful.

Wilburn owned a rental house and one of the neighbors came down with cancer and was having a hard time. Wilburn let them live in the rental house a long time rent free. This was Bobby Seagle, his wife and two daughters.

He always supported the Church. He never missed unless sometimes other things had to be done. He worked and retired at the Aluminum Company of America. Sometimes they had to work on Sunday especially during World War II.

He inherited the name "big smoke." He smoked real strong tobacco, me and my boys would ride to Church with him when Bethel was at work. One time on our way, my son Joe said, "Roll that window down and see if I can see how to get my breath." His wife Dorothy was a real Church worker, she died several years before Wilburn.

Their youngest daughter Jo Ann who married Raymond Ownby, adopted a son-Paul.

Paul was in an automobile and bicycle accident on Goose Gap Road and got killed. A little later, Jo Ann had a heart attack and died. Wilburn owned several acres of land which he left to his daughter Iva Helton King. Wilburn died June 10, 1997. Age 80. Wilburn, Dorothy, Jo Ann and Paul are buried in Mountain View Baptist Church Cemetery.

1st Timothy 4:8 "For bodily exercise profiteth little, but Godliness is profitable unto all things, having promises of the life that now is, and of that which is to come."

My brother Eliga Andrew Helton

Eliga Andrew Helton. Born February 25, 1919 to William Andrew Helton and Haretta Caroline Ward Helton. October 30, 2000. Age 81.

Eliga was fourth in the family of eleven children. Five brothers, Mack David, Hugh Wilburn, Charles Hubert, Reece, and Lynn Allen. Five sisters, Mary I. Zora, Nellie Lea, Callie Juanita, Olivia Ellender and Annice. His parents were farmers who was fortunate enough to raise enough food to feed a family of thirteen. By hard work and pulling together they made it just fine living in a four room house using every inch wisely.

When Eliga reached the right age He joined the C.C.C. at Tremont and Elkmont located near Gatlinburg in the Great Smoky Mountains. He stayed there until health problems arose. He was ruptured and unable to do hard work, so to survive he became a salesperson selling Watkins products. They sold various things such as liniments, soaps, pie filling and so on. I think I was inspired by his selling ability to become a Avon lady for over forty years.

Back in 1941 December 7, the United States declared war on Japan after they bombed Pearl Harbor. Many boys were drafted into service. We were surprised that Eliga passed because of his disability. But they were taking every able bodied person available. Even some who volunteered was only sixteen years old.

Eliga's surgery was not done until the war was over and he went to the V.A. Hospital in Johnson city where they almost mistook him for a patient who was to have his leg taken off. Lucky Eliga was not so groggy he could tell them they had the wrong patient. Eliga was inducted into the

Army at Fort Oglethorpe, Georgia. He took boot camp at Camp Polk, Louisiana. While there he met his future wife Myrtle Hall.

The war was raging and he was sent to Germany then on to Guadalcanal. Eliga was in battle at the Rhine river when they blew it up. Many was killed. Eliga said they thought as they looked back that they would never live to come back. Eliga was a medic caring for the wounded.

Back home, mom and dad and all us kids would listen for news on the radio for any word on where he might be and what might be happening.

One of us kids was at the mailbox every day looking for a letter or a card from him. My mother had very few grey hairs when he left but by the time the war was over and he came home her hair was almost all grey.

My dad's brother, Johnny, had four boys in the army: Bill Helton, Arthur Helton, Oscar Helton and Clyde Helton. All the brothers lived to make it back home except the youngest, Clyde Helton. He was killed, they buried him over there but a few years later they brought his body back to Sevierville, Tennessee and buried him at his home Church cemetery, Mountain View Baptist Church Cemetery. While all this was going on, my mom and dad were farmers working out in the heat. Worrying and working, dad had a heat stroke which damaged his health.

When Eliga went into the service, he knew the needs of his family. He made an "allotment" made possible by the U.S.A. where a amount of money would be sent to his family every month. Plus, he sent money from his monthly pay back to his family but mom and dad never spent one cent for their own use, only at Christmas time. Eliga wrote home and said "mom and dad please get all the kids something for Christmas." So they did.

So when the war was finally over and Eliga got to come home, the money which he truly deserved was safe in the Sevier County Bank in Eliga's name. Eliga sent money to California for Myrtle to come on a train to Knoxville, Tennessee so they could be married. The money came in handy for a soldier could buy a small truck and tractor, a few acres of land and a small house in Sevier County, Tennessee where he started his family with Myrtle Hall.

P.S. I remember Eliga getting a furlough while he was in the army Seems like he was alway interested in what we would like instead of thinking of himself. He borrowed a truck from our brother Mack and took us kids for a ride. I remember we passed another vehicle on a one lane bridge. Back then brakes on a car was not very good so they had to gear it down, but anyway, we made it safe back home.Happy to be with our brother Eliga there personally.

Another day in my life of eighty seven years that I remember was not only the saddest day but one of my happiest days.

It was Christmas night after World War II had ended. The war had ended three months before and we had not heard from Eliga. Back then we had no telephones in our homes in East Tennessee. It was a cold night Christmas day, the children who had married had brought their families and spent Christmas at mom and dad's. It had got late and the young kids had got sleepy and needed to be put to bed.

Eliga was on everyone's mind, a large box of cookies which had been bought three months before was still on a table in the back room. No one had mentioned it, we was all thinking, will Eliga ever make it back home? Then there was a noise on the steps and the shuffle of feet, my mother called out, "that's Eliga." We all rushed for the door but mom brushed us all back and Eliga was in her arms. That was the happiest day of my life, our brother was safe home.

 Myrtle and Eliga soon married and started their home in Sevier County, Tennessee Where they started their family, David Allen, Larry Wayne, Tommy, Shirley Louise. Eliga worked and retired at Rohm Haas Chemical Company in Knoxville. Eliga and Myrtle bought and moved to a large farm on 411 Highway in Blount County. They spent many happy years there. Myrtle, Eliga and their oldest son, David have passed away and is buried in Blount County at their home Church cemetery Prospect Baptist Church cemetery. The three younger children, Mr. and Mrs. Larry Wayne Helton, Mr. and Mrs. Tommy Helton, and Shirley Louise live on the Helton farm.

This is a note Eliga sent me in his later years:

There's a place within our hearts where memories abound. Where glimpses of our loved ones and happy days are found. We only have to go there to find strength, to carry on. And realize our loved ones are never really gone.

From Eliga and his girlfriend, Juanita Rayfield.

My sister Nellie Lea Helton

Born October 9, 1921.

Nellie was about nine years older than me. I remember as a child and on through life she was a great help to me. She tried to shield me from anything that might harm me. We grew up in hard times. We had few luxuries but we found there is treasures to be found in heartaches.

When she could earn a little money she would do without and buy me things. On thing always stands out in my mind. She bought me a pair of brown and white saddle oxford slippers. No other girl in our community had saddle oxfords. They lasted for years. I took good care of them keeping them cleaned and polished. She had a job keeping house for a family who lived in Knoxville, she would stay from Sunday evening until Friday evening.

I would always watch the road for her to come in sight and I would fly to meet her. Sometimes I would be naughty and my mom have to paddle me. I think it hurt Nellie more than me. Nellie had a harder time in life than I did. Before she married and after, she was wrongfully treated many times. My dad was more strict on the other kids than he was on the younger ones. I think he was afraid one of us would get in trouble and he wouldn't be able to get us out. But in his older years he loosened up. Out of all us children only one was arrested. That was Mack, the oldest and dad arrested him.

Mack was working at Elkmont for the C.C.C. Someone from our community picked him and two or three more up to bring them home who had alcohol with them. All of them started drinking, they brought Mack and let him out near where we lived at Bluff Mountain School, where our church was having church service.

When Mack got out of the car he said gosh, they're having church. I've got to get in there. It was cold and they had a pot bellied stove heating the building. Mack was cold and went up close to the stove and soon got warm and was vomiting. My mom and dad and small kids was at home, but someone ran out there and told dad, so as quick as he could he went out and got Mack, "made a citizen's arrest," brought him home and put him to bed.

A little time passed and someone knocked on our porch. It was Bill Huff, a constable, an officer of the law. He said I've come to get Mack. Dad said you can't have him. Bill had a blackjack and started beating on the porch and talking loud. "Scared us kids to death!" But dad wouldn't let him have Mack.

Early next morning dad got Mack up and took him over to Fox's Store located on the intersection of Goose Gap Road and Walden's Creek Road where "Bas" J.E. Sutton, who was a Justice of the Peace, and made him submit to disturbing the peace and paid a small fine. Everyone in our neighborhood was our friends. Mack was embarrassed to death but that learned him a lesson.

When we was young, we always walked to church and school along with our neighbors.

Nellie married Wilford Watson June 17, 1942. They had four children. Carolyn Ann, William Homer "Bill", Linda Lea and Jack Wilford. I was lucky enough to get to stay with her for two weeks when two of her children were born. Wilford worked at Rohm & Haas and they had bought a new home in Knoxville.

Wilford and my husband Bethel Crisp was good friends and Wilford helped Bethel get a job at Rohm & Haas. They both retired there "a well paying job with a good retirement." After Nellie and I was married for a short time we got to live close together out of one yard and into another. During that time our dad got cancer, before he died, me and Nellie would take time about keeping each other's children while the other one went to sit with dad.

Time passed and her and her family moved back to Knoxville. Wilford started having health problems and eventually had to retire. They bought property on Douglas Lake and sold their home in Knoxville and moved to the lake.

They always went back to church at Mountain View. It was on a Wednesday night June 8, 1972 they was on their way home from church, before they got to Sevierville Wilford had a heart attack and died. He was age forty eight. He is buried in the Mountain View Baptist Church cemetery. Nellie tried to live on the lake by herself and all the children was married. One day she told me I have come to the conclusion I cannot live up here by myself. Most of the people who lived up there was vacationing, partying or drinking. It was not safe for her.

My mom's house in Goose Gap was empty so Nellie moved into it and stayed until she bought property at Seymour, Tennessee near her son Jack and had a new house built. Shortly after Wilford died she went to work at Sevier Industries in Sevierville. She worked there until she retired. Nellie never cared about traveling and vacationing, watching movies, sports, soap operas. She always raised a garden, had a beautiful garden with all kinds of flowers and shrubs. She canned all kinds of vegetables and fruits, made jams and jellies.

 In the winter she quilted quilts, embroidered pillow slips for all the children and grandchildren. At Christmas time she made each one of us sisters a fancy sweatshirt pressing beautiful poinsettias on them. I have had mine for years and money couldn't buy it. When the weather gets cold I get it out and wear it; it's pretty warm.

 "She wants nothing to do with men period." Bill, her oldest son always looks out for her especially after she passed eighty. He would come and take her to the grocery store, ask her to come and live with him or he would come and live with her. But she would always say, let's just keep things like they are for now. She never wanted to be in the way.

 Bill got cancer and went to the hospital and had his kidney taken out and got better for awhile but the cancer came back and he died and is buried in the Mountain View Baptist Church cemetery. Bill was a awful good boy. He was one of my favorites.

 Nellie got the shingles which really took a toll on her life. Then she got dementia and one day she fell there at home By herself and when Jack found her he had to take her to the hospital and she was never able to come home anymore. She is in the nursing home, Asbury Place 2648 Sevierville Road near Maryville. Nellie never realized Bill had died. Nellie is a precious sister to me but I realize God knows best. I am sure he has control over all things. Wilford was licensed to preach January 8, 1969 by Mountain View Baptist Missionary Baptist Church.

1st. Corinthians 2:9 Eye hath not seen, ears have not heard, neither hath it entered into the heart of man, what God has in store for those who love and seek him.

My sister Callie Juanita born April 6, 1924

Juanita was five years older than me. She was so easy to get along with. She would let anyone do her dirty and never take up for herself. On her eighteenth birthday she gave birth to her son Jerry Olin Helton. He only lived one day. He is the 3rd person to be buried in the Mountain View cemetery.

When Juanita was very young there was two boys who wanted to marry her. That was H.C. Charles Minton and James Abbot. She liked both of them but she had briefly saw Grady Lowe, even though they didn't have a conversation she fell in love with him. It was over eight years before they finally met and she married the love of her life, April 16, 1946.

He was working at The Aluminum Company of America at Alcoa, Tennessee. In order for them to be together day and night he quit working at Alcoa and went to work where she worked weaving pocket books on a loom. They made it fine and soon bought ten acres of land which had a house and a barn on it on Goose Gap Road, Sevierville, Tennessee.

Their daughter Brenda Sue was born January 22, 1947. Their second daughter Patricia Juanita was born May 22, 1952.

I always felt sure if for any reason I needed a home to go to, along with my three sons, I would be welcome at Juanita and Grady's home. Grady was a member at Mountain View Missionary Baptist Church. He died with cancer December 1, 1967 at the age of 51. He is buried in the Mountain View Missionary Baptist Church cemetery.

Years later Charles H.C. Minton, who had went up north to work, heard that Juanita's husband Grady, had died. He came back to Tennessee and talked her into marrying him July 21, 1973. He treated her like dirt. She worked at KMart in Sevierville. He took advantage of her, opened his own business on her property, sold her land in Hidden Mountains that was supposed to be her daughters. He got a loan by putting a lien on everything she had borrowing money at the bank.

Charles H.C. had a hard childhood. His father left him and his mother, one brother and two sisters in the coal mines of Kentucky when the children were very young. His uncle brought them to Goose Gap in Sevierville, Tennessee and they lived in a little one room log house with a dirt floor.

They were at the mercies of the people who lived around them. There was no TennCare or relief. It was depression years and all the neighbors was scrambling to keep food on their own table. So all that had an effect on Charles H.C. Anyway, Juanita told me his mother, Maranda Minton was the best mother in law she ever had. Charles H.C. was a member at Mountain View Missionary Baptist Church. He got cancer and died June 12, 1993 and is buried near Grady in the Mountain View Missionary Baptist Church cemetery.

Juanita continued working at KMart. One day a man came in and spoke to her and she said hello. He said you don't know me? She said no. He said, it's been sixty years, I'm James Abbott or "Curly, you called me." I've been through World War II and stayed in the military, but I still want to marry you. Some time passed and James Roy Abbott married her October 29, 1996.

James wanted her to quit work and let him pay her debt off. But she said no, I got myself in this mess and I will get myself out of it. So she worked on at KMart until she was debt free.

James done everything he could for her, he treated her girls, Brenda and Pat like they were his own. He owned property in Pigeon Forge and left it to them. Everytime he got paid, he gave Star, Juanita's granddaughter money. Even after he got sick he told Juanita, every time my check comes you be sure my girls get their part. He bought Juanita a new Toyota car. He left his church membership at Smithwood Baptist Church because it was a small church and they needed his tithes and support.

James died and is buried in Smoky Mountain Memorial Gardens, Pigeon Forge, Tennessee. He was a good man.

Juanita is the only one in our family who married three times. We tease her and say anyone would have to be brave to marry you because you have already buried three husbands. She is our sister and we all love her. I know it would be hard to lose three husbands. She is 93 years old, her health is good and her mind is excellent. Everytime I want to know about things that happened years ago, "I call her." Grady was a #1 brother in law and so was James Abbott.

Read the Scripture: Ruth 1: 6-10.

My brother Charlie Hubert Helton

Charlie was almost four years older than me and he could whip the hide off me unless I could get my fighting shoes on. The shoes was made of "pigskin," kind of bumpy. They was not slippers like I would have liked them to have been, they was shoes and so ugly. I thought I would never wear them out but they came in handy when me and Charlie got into it, which was not very often. Mom and dad kept a close eye on us. He was born between me and my sister Juanita, who would never take up for herself. I was completely opposite, but anyway, we all got along pretty good.

A new family moved into our community and one of the boys was at church talking about us. He said you better not fool with them Helton's, there's too many of them. They all stick together. When Charlie was nine years old and in the fifth grade in school he had a sickness called "Acute Nephritis" having extremely sensitive sharp quick pain relating to inflammation of the kidneys, causing convulsions, to move or shake violently. We lived back in the country, never going to the doctor. We thought he was dying. My uncle George who lived close by jumped on a mule and went to Sevierville to get a doctor. Meanwhile, us kids was at school which was close by. Someone came to get us. When we got home, the yard was full of neighbors. The picture is still in my mind like it was yesterday. My mom was in the kitchen with baby Annice laying face down in her lap crying. My dad was at the barn praying. At that time dad had not been saved but he knew that the Lord was the only one who could help us.

A new family had moved into our community and the lady who was there, she knew Charlie was having convulsions. She put a spoon in his mouth and held it till he could not chew his tongue. When the doctor finally got there, he said Charlie had acute nephritis. We was told Charlie would have a short life. When he got well enough to go back to school, he had lost his memory and could not say his A.B.Cs. He studied hard and overcame that. He married Wilma Roberts February 11, 1946. They have one son, James Hubert Helton. Charlie worked and retired from The Aluminum Company of America.

There are four generations in Charlie's family who worked on the railroads. First, my dad, William Andrew Helton worked on the train that ran between Knoxville and Sevierville, Charlie worked at the roundhouses at Alcoa switching and fueling and so on. Charlie's son Hubert worked and retired on the Norfolk Southern Railway. Now, Smoky, Hubert's son has been retired at the same Norfolk Southern Railway "A whole lot of Smoking a going on." I guess if the truth be told, Charlie could buy and sell all of us other ten children. He is 90 years old and lives by himself. He accomplished that by putting his mind and body to work.

My Brother Reese Helton.

My brother Reece Helton born November 18, 1932. Died July 11, 2012.

Reece was born when I was three years old. We was always close. All his life he always put others first, even when he was young he would give his toys or anything he had to others. I think he was the easiest child to raise mom and dad had. Even when dad got cancer and knew he was going to die, he called Reece up to his bed and told him to take care of mom "A hard job" but Reece done his best as he did in many of his life's jobs.

Reece served in the U.S. Army and spent time overseas operating a crane there at the Rhine River, during World War II. My brother Eliga was there when it was bombed and blew the place off the map. I remember Eliga telling me his regiment had just crossed the river when the enemy blew the bridge up. He said they looked back and saw a sight that would always be stamped on their mind. They thought they would never make it back home, but they did and years later Reece was over there operating a crane helping rebuild the bridge. Through Reece's life he rebuilt many bridges naturally and mentally.

Reece married Lillie Mae Suttles November 23, 1956. They have four children. Deborah, Steve, Karen and Judy. Reece attended Mountain View Baptist Church from birth on. Our Mother took him there when he was a baby, he was saved there and joined the church. Through the years he attended church there and worked as music director, teacher, trustee, janitor, and cemetery caretaker. He was known all over Sevier and surrounding counties for his singing and harp music.

He was once voted commissioner in Sevier County. He did not run but had enough write in votes to be elected. He served that year and they asked him to run the next year but he told me it was very hard to be in politics and be a Christian.

He was the caretaker over the cemetery at Mountain View for several years. I know he replaced four or five tombstones that had no names or dates, especially in the Shiloh cemetery near Henderson's Chapel Baptist Church in Sevier County. He worked hard trying to get people to stay in church. He was always looking for little jobs to get weak Christians interested in to keep them in church. "He was a light in a dark place."

As years passed he got Parkinson Disease and was in Sevier County Nursing Home. My sister Annice and I would try to visit him every time we could. One day when I went to visit he told me the man who had helped him with his bath told him he was the only patient there who owned an electric toothbrush. He said he told him I had come a long way from a willow twig to an electric toothbrush. I told him to tell him the next time, I have come a long way from a Sears & Roebuck Catalog to a roll of Charmin tissue.

In years past I would sit with him on the front bench in church. One Sunday I took out a piece of gum and put it in my mouth and offered him one. He said I don't chew gum in church. "The tone of his voice told me I shouldn't either." Reece was a very good friend and brother in law to my husband Bethel C. Crisp. He would always visit the church Bethel was pastoring and bring his quartet and sing when we was having special services and revivals. There was no better brother than Reece Helton. One of his favorite scriptures was Ephesians 6:10 "Put on the whole armour of God, that ye may be able to stand against the wiles of the devil."

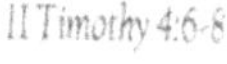

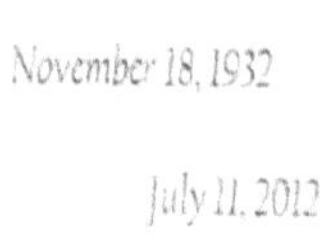

My sister Annice Helton

Born February 16, 1935. Married December 4, 1953 to Charles Huskey.

Annice was the youngest girl in the family of eleven children and the only one of the girls not to have a middle name. We meant for it to be Annice Lela, the Lela was after a school teacher we had at Bluff Mountain School. Lela King Gobble was a excellent teacher, but when Annice's birth certificate came back it only said Annice Helton. Annice was eighteen when she met and married Charles Huskey. They have three children. Peggy Lynn, "Chuckey" Charles and "Nick" Nicholas Paul.

Peggy married Rod Garrett and they have two sons. Chuck married Doranda and they have two children. Amanda Makala and John Paul. Nick never married. Charles Huskey died of cancer December 23, 1992. 59 years old.

Years later Annice met and married Jack Rogers April 21, 2001. Annice worked and retired at Cherokee Textile Mills. She has been a caregiver to her son Nick for over twenty seven years who was injured while hospitalized and paralyzed from his neck down.

Annice lived near me and our Mom. In Mom's later years she was a great help to her. She has also lives near me and since my husband Bethel Crisp died, she and her husband, Jack Rogers are a great help to me. If I am going to be out of my house or gone from home, I always let Annice know. Jack is always ready to help any way he can. If I want to put out a few things in his garden he lets me. And Nicholas who is not comfortable around some people told Annice when Bethel died to tell me he had a extra bed in his apartment I could sleep in. He said I didn't need to be by myself and afraid. I know Nick really loves me or he would not have said that. Annice is my beautician. She has cut my hair for years. Annice takes no time for herself. She is always thinking of others. "I salute her for a job well done."

My brother "Manker" Lynn Allen Helton

Born July 16, 1938.

Lynn Allen was the last of the siblings born to mom and dad. When my dad went out to work, he said we got a new baby at our house, it's a boy. Even though he already had five boys he was so proud he had another one. The whole family was proud. I remember I was age nine, just the right age to babysit. I loved my job. It made me feel grown up that mom would leave me in charge of him when she had to go about her chores but she would never go out of a hollering distance.

Lynn was always easy to care for. One thing, he was healthy, hardly ever had a bad cold or anything.

When he started school, the school, "Bluff Mountain School" was a very short distance from home. We always came home for lunch.

I remember when dad started building our new house. My uncle Charlie Shular who lived in Knoxville and was a good carpenter "Him and my dad were good friends" he also had a brother, Manker Shular, they would come on Saturday and help dad get the house under roof so that dad with the help of mom and all us kids could finish the house.

During that time Lynn Allen took up with Manker Shular and named himself "Manker Lynn Allen." He has proudly carried that name Manker Lynn Allen all his life. Lynn always done well with the companies he worked for "some of them very interesting." Anyway, he is in bad health and has cancer, parkens, sleep apnea and other things. He married Betty Jo Holland October 26, 1956. They have three children: Jo Anna Lynn, (Bill) Reverend William

Ronald Eugene and Patricia Juanita. "There is no better family."

Betty Jo has several health problems but they all work together like a family should. Sometimes when Betty Jo has a doctor's appointment and Jo Anna has to take her, me and my sister Juanita gets to go and sit with Lynn. We really enjoy that. I keep my ears open hearing about interesting things that happened back when Bethel and I lived at Seymour.

Lynn, Betty Jo, Bill and his family and Jo Anna lives on Mortar Branch Road, Sevierville, Tennessee on the farm that dad owned years ago. After my dad died, Lynn Allen bought the place from my mom. It is property where years ago Mortar Branch School was held there. There was a cistern, a man made well for holding rain water underground in the school yard. Years ago there was two of those in the community. The other one was on the Jim Whaley place at Goose Gap and Spring Holler Road. "Very dangerous thing."

Lynn Allen and his son Bill got saved one week apart at Mountain View Baptist Church. They immediately joined the Church and was baptized. Bill was soon called to preach and the Church ordained him. He has pastored different Churches including Mountain View. Lynn is a ordained deacon, Betty Jo was the Church clerk and they were the Church janitor until health problems made them unable. Even though they are unable, they still send their tithes to the Church.

Hebrews Chapter 12:1-2.

"Therefore seeing we are also compassed about with so great a cloud of witnesses, let us lay aside every weight, and the sin which doth so easily beset us, and let us run

with patience the race that is set before us .Looking unto Jesus the author and finisher of our faith, who for the joy that was set before him endured the cross, despising the shame, and is set down at the right hand of God.
Bill Helton preached this Scripture April 11, 2014 at Mountain View Easter Sunday.

In Reference Of Reece Helton

I wonder if the savior spent A day or two with you
Would you go right on doing the things you always do?

Would you keep right on saying the things you always say?
Would life for you continue as it does from day to day?

Would your family conversation keep up its usual pace
And would you find it hard each meal to say a table grace?

Would you sing the songs you always sing and read the
Books you read. And let him know the things on which
Your mind and spirit feed?
Would you take Jesus with you Everywhere youd planned to go?
Or would you maybe change your plans For just a day or so?
Would you be glad to have him meet Your very closest friends.
Or would you hope theyd stay away Until His visit ends?
Would you be glad to have him stay Forever on and on.
Or would you sigh with great relief When He at last was gone?
It might be interesting to know The things that you would do,

If Jesus Christ in person came To spend some time with you.

RATTLESNAKE GOSPEL for JACOB JOB

Way down in the State of Old Kentuck,
The hardest place that e'er was struck,
There lived a man named Jacob Job,
The meanest on this mundane globe.

He cared not for God or man,
Except his wild and wicked clan.
He had six boys, both big and bad,
Who followed right behind their dad.

They drank that Wildcat Whiskey down,
And painted red the country town.
He had six daughters, buxom gals,
Who danced and capered with their pals.

They laughed and frolicked o'er the hills
And, sometimes, tippled at the stills.
Then, one day an awful rattlesnake
Bit the oldest boy, Big Wicked Jake.
And through his veins the poison flew;
"He's going to die, what can we do?"

They sent a runner to the town
To fetch in haste, old Parson Brown;
A Dutchman of John Wesley's band,
As fine as any in the land.

He prayed a curious, wondrous prayer,
With words of faith and wisdom rare.
Whether in heaven it reached or not,
On earth it surely hit the spot.

Oh Gott, we thank Thee for dis snake.
that thou has sent to bite old Jake.
To fetch him down from his high hoss,
and lead him to the savior's cross.

He would not mend his wicked way,

until kind providence today.
Now oh Lord the great I AM.
Please send another to bite old Sam

And Jock and Shawn, der vurst of rakes,
Oh, Gott! we need more rattlesnakes!
And send de biggest on the globe
To bite ole Pappy, Jacob Job.

And his vife, she need vun too;
Perhaps a copperhead vould do.
And chicken snakes to bite the gals,
and all dere dancing, vicked pals.

And now, Oh Gott before too late,
Please hurry up dose Gospel snakes,
And safe dis ole Kentucky State,
And hear dis prayer for Jesus sake. Amen
Jacob Job 1737-1808

This poem is older than my grandparents by many generations. It is also known as The
Dutchman's Prayer. It was sent to me by an old Jobe, as told to her by another old
Jobe...funny how that happens.
Randy

There is two Ways to Cross
a Mountain,
Climb it or go around it.
but if you take the easy way, you
will miss the view from the top

Russ Hilton

51

Come little leaves said the Wind one day
Come over in the meadow with me and play
put on your Coat of yellow and gold
for summer has gone and the days grow cold
Dancing and flying the little leaves went
Winter had Come and they were Content,
Soon they were fast in their beds
Snow lay a blanket over them here,

Twinkle, twinkle little star,
How I wonder where you are,
Up above the world so high
Like a diamond in the sky.
When the blazing sun is set
And the grass with dew is wet
Then you show your better light
Twinkle, twinkle, all the night

"A Way to be saved"

Life doesn't work when we ignore God +
Selfishly insist on doing things our way.
The bible calls this sin. At this point
we need a remedy.

Now that you have heard the good news, God
wants you to respond to him; you can talk
to him   Using words like these. My life is
broke, I recognise it because of my sin,
I believe Christ Come to live, die, and was
raised from the dead to rescue me from
my sins. "Forgive Me" I turn from my
selfish ways and put my trust in you.
I know that Jesus is Lord of all, and I will
follow him
   " We must ask God to forgive us "
Philippians 2:13   Ephesians 2:10

The reward of faithfulness Comes with the
expectation of Continued Obedience

Matthew 19:1-12; Mark 10:2-12

Have you seen any copy of a marriage ceremony?

Look at the one printed below. Read it carefully and then list the promises each makes.

A Marriage Ceremony

Dearly beloved, we are gathered together here in the sight of God, and in the face of this company, to join together this man and this woman in holy matrimony.

Marriage is a joyous occasion. It is connected in our thoughts with the magic charm of home, and with all that is pleasant and attractive in the tenderest and most sacred relations of life.

When celebrated in Cana of Galilee, it was sanctioned and cheered by the presence of the Lord himself; and it is declared by an inspired Apostle to be honorable in all.

And now, if you, John Jones and Ann Wood, have at present appeared for the purpose of being joined in legal wedlock, you will please to signify this intention by uniting your right hands.

John, do you take the lady whom you now hold by the hand to be your lawful and wedded wife? (He answers, "I do.")

Do you promise to love and cherish her, in sickness and in health, for richer for poorer, for better for worse, and forsaking all others keep thee only unto her, so long as you both shall live? (He answers, "I do.")

Ann, do you take the gentleman who now stands by your side and who holds you by the hand, to be your lawful and wedded husband? (She answers, "I do.")

Do you promise to love and cherish him, in sickness and in health, for richer for poorer, for better for worse, and forsaking all others, keep thee only unto him, so long as you both shall live? (She answers, "I do.")

Do you mutually promise in the presence of God, and of these witnesses, that you will at all times and in all circumstances, conduct yourselves toward one another as becometh husband and wife? (Both answer, "I do.")

That you will love, cherish, and adhere to one another, until separated by death. (Both answer, "I do.")

(Then the ring ceremony is said if the couple desires to include this as a part of the ceremony. The groom and the bride will each in turn repeat these words after the minister, a phrase at a time.)

With this ring I thee wed; in the name of the Father, and of the Son, and of the Holy Ghost. Amen. (Then the minister concludes:)

Having taken these pledges of your affection and vows of your fidelity, I do therefore, by authority of the laws of this state, sanctioned by divine authority, pronounce you, John Jones and Ann Wood, lawfully married, husband and wife; in the name of the Father, and of the Son, and of the Holy Ghost. What, therefore, God hath joined together, let not man put asunder.

<table>
<tr><td>(Only the girls write these)
Promises the Bride Makes</td><td>(Only the boys write these)
Promises the Groom Makes</td></tr>
<tr><td>1.
2.
3.
4.</td><td>1.
2.
3.
4.</td></tr>
</table>

DO NOT JUDGE TOO HARD

Pray do not find fault with the man
 That limps or stumbles along the road;
Unless you have worn the shoes he wears,
 Or struggled beneath his load.
There may be tacks in his shoes that hurt,
 Though hidden away from view;
Or the burdens he bears placed on your back,
 Might cause you to stumble, too.

Don't sneer at the man who is down today,
 Unless you have felt the blow
That caused his fall, or felt the pain
 That only the fallen know.
You may be strong, but still the blows
 That were his, if dealt to you
In the selfsame way at the selfsame time
 Might cause you to stagger, too.

Don't be too hard on the man who sins,
 Or pelt him with words or a stone,
Unless you are sure, doubly sure,
 That you have no sins of your own.
For you know, perhaps, if the tempters voice
 Should whisper as soft to you
As it did to him when he went astray,
 It might cause you to falter, too.

Author Unknown

Olivia and Bethel

Bethel Crisp came over from Andrews North Carolina to work at Alcoa Aluminum Company in Blount County and met Olivia Helton on Goose Gap Road, Sevierville, Tennessee. They were married October 9, 1947 in Blairsville, Georgia. They first lived in a log house rented from Sally Howk on Mortar Branch Road, later moved next door to a house owned by Olivia's father.

While living there, July 28, 1948 their son James William was born and Howard Donald was born August 9, 1949. From there they moved to the 10th district in Sevier County on Arthur Oakley's farm, a big house on several acres of land. We were the caretakers. There was horses, cattle, pigs, chickens, a tractor and farm machinery. We had a big garden, a tobacco crop, we stayed there around two years and decided to go to Detroit, Michigan "to get rich." Several young men and their families from Sevier County had gone up there to work in the car factories. When we left Sevierville we had a good home, access to the farm and all it had to offer and a little money in the Sevier County Bank. Living in Michigan was completely different from Tennessee. There was alcohol everywhere. We did not go to church one time. On weekends we would visit parks and our friends who had moved up there and sometimes we would drive over into Canada.

Anyway, we stayed a little over a year and came back to Tennessee broke. We moved into my dad's rental house on mortar Branch and lived there until my brother Wilburn sold us four acres of land at a good price and let us build a house and pay later. Me and Bethel practically built the house. My brother Reece would help us when we run into something we couldn't handle. During that time, Bethel went to work at Rohm and Haas in Knoxville. Joe was born February 18, 1955. James and Howard started school at Bluff Mountain School on Goose Gap Road, Sevierville, Tennessee. The school was in sight of where we lived.

Bethel got laid off from Rohm and Haas, my brother Eliga sold us a strip of land on Goose Gap Road right across the road from the school. He also sold us a small building and helped Bethel move it onto the property. So we fixed it up and opened up a Jottum Down Store. There was no other store on Goose Gap Road. In that little store we had just about everything anybody needed. We had jobbers who came by once a week, Coke men and breadmen. We sold meal, flour, salt, soda, baking powder, bread, cakes, kerosene, motor oil, etc. People came by and ate lunch, then we sold them bologna and cheese sandwiches, moon pies, cokes and icecream.

James and Howard was in school just across the road. Joe was young and first stayed in a lay down stroller, then when he got older in a playpen. Every cent the school children got they spent it at our store. We had the first T.V. on Goose Gap Road. We had a lot of company come by just to see what it was like.

By this time Bethel had got called back to Rohm and Haas and had started going to church with me and the boys. Mountain View Church had called a new preacher, Earl Wilhoit who lived on Allensville Road out from Sevierville and was a genuine Christian. He had corrected Bethel on a thing or two when he was out in sin and time passed and they became lifelong friends. The next preacher we had was Loren Whaley from Wears Valley. He came and brought his family. Loren had a way about his preaching to lead people to Christ. Bethel got saved and was called to preach and real soon Waldens Creek Baptist Church called him to be their pastor. Mountain View Church ordained him. I was concerned whether I could be a worthy preacher's wife. I prayed a lot and again the Lord had some good people there who made me feel loved and needed.

As we went to other churches, God always filled our need. We met many people who became lifelong friends. During all this time Bluff Mountain School was closing and moving all the children to Benson School on Waldens Creek Road. We had been looking for and found property and a home on Nails Creek "now Burnett Station." That property was cornered on Knox, Sevier and Blount County. A ideal place for a preacher to live and have access to churches in those three counties plus Rohm and Haas (his work place).

For a brief time before moving to Seymour James and Howard went to Sevierville Elementary School. Shortly after we moved Bethel was called to Burnetts Creek Baptist Church in Knox County. Our son James was saved there. Seymour was a good place to live. The school bus ran right past our yard. We had one of the best bus drivers in the county, Wayne Campbell, he was also a Methodist minister. He would always blow his horn and wait while the kids would grab a biscuit and some of their clothing and finish getting ready on the bus.

There was a good man named Rowe King who was interested in children. He would get up a ball team and pick them up for practice and games, "Charging nothing." They had a real good team. James and Howard had a lot of fun and saw a good example in Rowe. I am sure Rowe King has been rewarded by the Lord for helping so many children.Howard had a donkey. Sometimes it would stub up and he would have to crank its tail.

We had very good neighbors, the Guffeys, Jim and Gladys, the Greens, Johnny and Jean, their daughter Brenda, Mr. and Mrs, Ed Bales, their son Pete, the Mize's, Jack and Virginia, their children Barbara, Jackie, Wayne and another daughter and many more. Those were the closest neighbors. Their children and grandchildren was our children's age so they became life long friends.

Our boys all went to Prospect Elementary School in Blount County. James and Howard went to Porter High School and James graduated there but by that time they had opened the Seymour School which was closer, so Howard and Joe graduated at Seymour High.

James attended Carson Newman, he didn't graduate. He was always a boy who wanted to stay close to home. James and Howard worked on weekends for Cas Walker who owned several grocery stores in East Tennessee.

James, Howard and Joe was always good boys helping around the house with all the chores. When they were little they was easy to take care of, they were no whiners, they helped around the house, never staying out late to worry us. They never grumbled when they had to go to church, Saturday night, Sunday morning, Sunday night, Wednesday night, every singing, every revival, they always helped mom and dad any way they could. The good Lord let them be born at a good time...before drugs. I am very blessed to have them.

Life is no small thing. The family I came into is no accident. There is gifts to be found in life's hardships and tragedies. I am blessed by being born into a good family. First, I am born to parents who tried to raise me right. I am blessed with six brothers, four sister, a husband of sixty seven years, three sons, three grandchildren, two great grandchildren, one great, great grandchild.

Matthew 11:28,29 "Come unto me all ye that labour and are heavy laden, and I will give you rest. Take my yoke upon you, learn of me, for I am meek and lowly in heart: and ye shall find rest for your souls."

Our fiftieth wedding anniversary.

On our fiftieth wedding anniversary we went to Hawaii. All my life I had dreamed of going to Hawaii but had no idea I would ever get to go. So as our fiftieth anniversary drew near, Bethel and our three boys decided we could go, so we made ready. I decided right away I was not taking valuables with me that I would have to worry about losing.

When we got to the ticket station they asked for a picture I.D, everyone looked at me. I said I didn't bring mine. The lady said you will have to have it, no way I could get back home to Sevierville from the Knoxville airport to get it. Just happened a lady at the ticket office knew us and talked them into letting me go. They said you can go but you won't get back. Anyway, we went and we had a wonderful time. But they went through our luggage a few times, the weather was just right, we saw no policemen. We asked about that. They told us, don't worry about that they are everywhere.

There was music and dancing everywhere; there were caves, waterfalls, we could even go up on the mountain and look down and see airplanes flying down below. The volcano's were everywhere. You could warm by them or you could get burned. The flowers were beautiful and blooming everywhere. Nearly all the ladies was wearing them up by their ear. When we was almost ready to come home, Paulette and I found out we was wearing them by the wrong ear, we was sending out the wrong message.

Bethel had been there when World War II was on, it brought back bad memories. He was there when news came to him his brother James had been killed in Belgium. We could see damage that had been done when the enemy had bombed Pearl Harbor.

James and Paulette went with us. They choose James and others to dance with the hula girls. James won the prize. September 12th, Big Island Volcano, that evening we flew to Maui. First Island we stayed at the Hyatt Honolulu. Waikiki Beach, Pearl Harbor, Dream Land Head, Dole Pineapple Plantation, State Capitol, King Kamana Palace and South Pacific. 15, 16 17, Kauai, Lighthouse, state park, Waimea Canyon,fern grotto luau, James dancing. I think my favorite thing was King Kamana Palace. We went to church there and the preacher had on a skirt. I didn't know what their denomination was.

Our boy's gave us a 50th wedding anniversary reception at Mountain View Baptist Church Fellowship Hall and invited friends and relatives. People came from near and far. "Life has been good."

My Mom

My mother, Haretta Caroline Ward Helton, daughter of Martha Ann Elizabeth Ward. My mother was born and raised in Knox County. I never knew my grandma Ward. She died about seven years before I was born. The cause of her death was, she had a "Boil" a very painful pus filled swollen area of the skin caused by bacteria in her temple which killed her. She was also blind in one eye caused by getting a sewing needle stuck in her eye when she was a young teenager.

She is buried in the Middle Creek Methodist Church cemetery. Mom's brother Oscar Ward married Mary Helton "My dad's sister." Their children were Luther, Oscar, Bruce, Roger and Alma. Her brother Mack who married Maggie Atchley, their children were Bill, Kenneth, Clyde 'Sunny." Her brother Lee who never married. Her brother Luther married Lesley.

As I have already said in my book, my mom and dad slipped off and got married. When my dad was nineteen and mom liked two days being fifteen, but she was made out of tuff stuff. She gave birth to all eleven kids with no doctors help and done a good job helping raise eleven children. She always saw that the house was clean and the meals was ready three times a day, plus, she took care of the garden, raised and canned all kinds of fruits and vegetables, drying fruit, canning pickles and berries, making jam and jellies and when the hogs was killed she rendered the lard two or three five gallon cans, made crackling bread. She took the meat scraps and made lye soap to wash the clothing. All the laundry had to be done at the spring where the iron wash kettle was set up. She was lucky to have a wash board. Some of the neighbors had to use a river rock.

She always got up early and started the fire in the fireplace and cook stove and had breakfast ready by the time dad had the horses fed and the kids was ready for school. She always had us clean clothing for school or whatever. She always milked two or three cows twice a day, churned the milk, made butter milk, butter and cottage cheese, took out the ashes from the fireplace and cook stove.

She had no idle time to sit and read or relax. She made most of our clothing only the overalls and boys pants. She pieced and quilted quilts "the cotton, she raised in the garden." She had cotton cards so she made batting, the quilt frames hung over the living room where she could lift it up and down. I tried to learn to quilt but I never could. I would always stick my finger.

While the older children went to school she kept busy watching the younger ones, working and gathering things from the garden, cooking dinner. The school was so close we could come home for lunch so there was no rest period. She had no cosmetics, only soap and water. She was always properly dressed. I don't ever remember seeing her in slacks or blue jeans. Her hair was naturally curly which she parted on one side, held back with a bobby pin, a little less than shoulder length. She had no jewelry.

As time passed and some of the children got older and got jobs and some married, we got the new house, one of the nicest in Goose Gap, a new barn, the biggest in Goose Gap, things got a little easier. Mom and dad always respected Sunday as the Lord's day, a day to go to church, not shooting firearms or firecrackers. Our friends or relatives from Sevierville and Knoxville come to visit on Sunday. Mom would kill a chicken and made cakes or pies on Saturday to have for Sunday dinner. Things got a little easier till my dad got cancer and with the help of us kids mom took care of him. There was no such thing as health insurance or nursing home. My dad died on October 25, 1952 at age 60.

Dad had asked Reece to take care of mom. When Reece married, his wife came to live and their family at the home place with mom. About fifteen years passed, a man, Lee Myers who him and his wife had lived in our community and raised their family had moved to Blount County closer to his workplace in Alcoa and his wife, Mamie Price was a church worker, she was my Sunday School teacher when I was young. Their daughter, Wilma Dean was my best friend. Lee's wife Mamie had died and all the children had married except one who was an invalid. Lee started coming back up to church at Mountain View.

One day we kids got a surprise. Lee Myers and his son Albert and his wife came up to Goose Gap and picked mom up and took her to Bryson City, North Carolina and mom and Lee got married. That was a shock that took awhile to get over, but everything turned out good. Lee treated mom like a baby. Everywhere you saw one of them you saw the other one. All his children treated her with respect. Occasionally they came and spent the weekend with me and my family and go to church with us. They attended church regularly near where they lived. On special occasions like decorations and home comings they came back to Mountain View Church.

As time passed, I would go on Tuesdays and visit and do some things around the house they were not able to do.

One day I said to Lee, "You just treat me like a step child." He looked at me for awhile and then laughed. I think that anything I would ask him to do for me he would have done it. We couldn't have had a better stepfather. There was never any friction between Lee and us kids. One night at suppertime Lee had a heart attack and was gone. Mom had a bad heart and had to go into Blount Memorial Hospital for a few days. When she recovered Reece wanted her to come back to the home place in Goose Gap and live with him and his family. But Eliga and Myrtle talked her into coming to live with them in Blount County. While living there she attended church at Prospect Baptist Church. Occasionally she would spend the weekend and go to church with the other children and some of her lifelong friends in Goose Gap.

My oldest sister Zora who had Lou Gehrig's disease died October 14, 1981 age 66. A short time later, February 5, 1982 at age 85 my mom died. She is buried with my Dad in Mountain View Baptist Church cemetery. The one who had spent her life from age fifteen giving birth and raising eleven children, making us feel safe and secure had finished her work and laid down her heavy load and went to glory land.

I am including the following article for my daughter in law Paulette. She teaches young children. She does everything for them and worries about them all the time.

Public Pulpit

Tommie & Susan

The little boy was dirty, made bad grades and had several fights. When it came time to give the teacher presents, some laughed and mocked when he gave her a broken bracelet and an opened bottle of perfume. She graciously put the bracelet on as well as a bit of perfume."You smell like my mom," Tommy Stoddard told her.

Curious, his teacher did some research on Tommy and read that in the first grade he was a good student and played well with others. But in the second year his mother died and he became withdrawn. By the third grade he had deteriorated further until he got to her class. After knowing his terrible difficulties, she began to take a special interest and encourage him.

Years later she got a note from him after graduating from high school, thanking her for being the best teacher he ever had. He wrote the same kind of note after college graduation and became a doctor. Then a few years later he invited her to his wedding, to sit where his mom would sit. She came, wearing the same bracelet and perfume.

Few children experience the death of a parent early, but many are abandoned by a womanizing dad or one on drugs, etc. If my dad or mom had bailed out in second grade, I had a battle axe for a teacher then, so I hate to think of what would have happened to me and my brother.

Parents, please try to work things out, and pray to be more irritated at your own sins than those of your spouse. Teachers and neighbors, pray God will show you a Tommie or a Susan, and how you can be a blessing and not a curse to them. And if you have received great encouragement from an adult when you were a child, let them know.

If that encouragement came from your parents, you can be certain they also would love to know they had good influence on you!

111

David Allen Helton

David Allen Helton who was more than a nephew.

David's father Eliga was my brother who had gone through World War II and had served overseas. While in Camp Polk, Louisiana he had met and fell in love with Myrtle Hall. Shortly after, Eliga was shipped overseas, Myrtle's mother died and Myrtle went to New York to live with her brother.

When the war was over and Eliga had come home, he sent for Myrtle to come to Tennessee and they were married. Shortly after they married Myrtle became pregnant and had a difficult pregnancy. Word came from Louisiana that her father had died. Eliga talked to her doctor and together they decided with the problem she was having she would not be able to go to the funeral in Louisiana. It would be best to wait until the baby was born before telling her. They waited, but Myrtle had a nervous breakdown anyway. David Allen was born December 25, 1946 in Sevierville, Tennessee.

When Myrtle was able to come home from the hospital, I went to stay with them and do things Myrtle was not able to do. Anyway, I always said David was my first baby, he was a very good and healthy baby. I was not a very good cook or housekeeper but with Eliga's help we made do. I wound up bringing David home with me at mom's and dad's. Myrtle was so nervous she could not take care of David. She told me that every time he started crying she wanted to take him up and throw him against the floor.

My mother helped me but I was mostly in charge of David, sleeping with him, fixing his bottle, bathing and changing him. All around, he was a good baby. Anyway, I had just met Bethel who had come over from North Carolina to work at Alcoa. Bethel's aunt Velma lived next door to us. Bethel had come to visit them and talked their son Oscar Dee into coming up to our house. I was in the kitchen when they came in the front door. A short time later, David, who was in the bedroom asleep, woke up and in order to get David I had to go through the living room where Bethel was. Well, I had on overalls and I had not combed my hair. I tried to get my sister Annice to go get David but she would not. I was afraid he would fall out of the bed so I went and got him bringing him back through the living room, barely speaking to Bethel and Oscar Dee.

Bethel could see my mom was to old and my sister Annice was too young, looked at Oscar Dee and said "who's baby is that?" Anyway, I did the best I could with David. There was a strong bond between us that lasted through life. His mother finally got able to take care of him. He got the short end of a lot of life's problems. The first day he went to elementary school he accidently got hit in the mouth with a ball bat knocking his two upper teeth out. He had to deal with that all his life. David graduated High School at Porter in Blount County. He later went to Hiwassee College then later joined the U.S. Air Force where he was sent to Vietnam. I am enclosing a paper clipping of some things that happened there.

DFC Given for Rescue in Vietnam

MARYVILLE, Feb. 29 (Special)—Sgt. David A. Helton of Maryville has been decorated at the Da Nang AB, Vietnam,

for what the Air Force describes as "his heroic actions during a dramatic sea rescue." He received the Distinguished Flying Cross.

Sgt. Helton, 21, remained behind in turbulent waters of the South China

Helton

Sea in his effort to rescue an injured fellow American.

Helton, an HH43 Huskie helicopter crewman, was on alert fire control duty when an F105 Thunderchief pilot was forced to eject in rough coastal waters off Da Nang.

As the Air Force copter hovered over the flier, Helton lowered the sling but the airman, who suffered broken legs, was unable to climb into it. Unhesitatingly, Helton jumped into the high swells to assist the injured man.

Then, when the airborne crew was unable to clear the pilot from the helicopter doorway because of his injuries, Helton voluntarily remained in the treacherous water as a second chopper was diverted to the area and Helton's copter departed for Da Nang. Within minutes, Helton was hoisted to safety.

Helton, a 1964 Porter High School graduate, is the son of Mr. and Mrs. Eliga A. Helton, Rt. 3, Maryville. Before entering the Air Force in March 1965, he attended Hiwassee College in Madisonville.

114

After he got discharged he got a job in Johnson City. There he met and married a lady he dearly loved. They had two children, Michelle and Michael. I never knew why they divorced. Time passed and David remarried. At Christmas time David went to spend some time with the children taking some Christmas gifts, came home and started putting up the Christmas decorations, started having chest pains, his wife went with him to St. Mary's Hospital in Knoxville. He got out at the Emergency door and walked in. His wife parked the car and went in, 'David was gone." Died December 10, 1990. David is buried in Prospect Baptist Church cemetery in Blount County with his mother and father. At David's burial, the U.S. Air Force sent planes and did a military salute at Prospect cemetery.

 Some time passed and his wife Patricia Odem Helton sent me and Bethel a nice card saying "I am not sending this for me, I am sending it for David, he dearly loved you." Patricia has since passed away and is buried with David at Prospect cemetery.

To My Other Mother

You are the Other Mother I received,
    The Day I Wed your Son

And I Want to Thank you Mom.
    For the loving things you've done,

You've given Me a gracious Man,
    With whom I share my life,

You are his ~~loving~~ lovely Mother
    And I his Lucky Wife.

You use to Pat his little head,
    And Now I hold his hand,

You Raised in Love a little Boy,
    And then gave me the Man,

From my Son James Wife Pautelle Williamson
                    Crisp

I watched Mommie and Daddy as they
Rolled them out the door
One by one they've left for Heaven
And their faces well see no more
But Jesus said it and I believe it.
that old grave has been defeated
Death Lost its sting when that old
stone was rolled away.
                    -Cho-
Thank God there's comeing a time And I know
  it wont be long, till Ill see them again
  in their new home
  there well be singing songs of gladness
  And well Never sleep no more
    when we got togiather one more time
    On Heavens shore
                    -2-
How I miss that old Preacher, Lord his face I
long to see. And I miss my old neighbor who
lived jeust down the road from me. but they are
resting from their labors. Never more to work and
toil, in the arms of Jesus they are safe
ever more

My Grandmow.

My Grandmow is 54 years old. I have lived with her for 16 years (I will Be 18 on June 3). She has always been there for me. As long as I have my Grandmow I Know I'm loved.

When We had the wreck this summer I almost lost her and my grandfather it made me realize how much I really love her. We used to fight alot, but not now. She still lets me Know when she dasent like someone, but she dont tell me not to see them.

In short I love my Grandmother very, very much, and I dont Know What I'll do when she is gone.

From My Granddaughter
Jennifer Louise C'risp

Our first grandchild

Jennifer Louise Crisp born June 3, 1969. Daughter of Howard Crisp and Barbara Garner.

Jennifer graduated from Sevier County High School, married Mark Christianer, had two children, Deven Caleb born November 3, 1989. Chase Wesley, born January 3, 1992.

Jennifer and Mark are now divorced. Jennifer died January 31, 2008 of cancer (leukemia). Buried in Mountain View Baptist Church cemetery. Chase Wesley was adopted by Jennifer's aunt and uncle Pattie and Robert Garner. His name is changed to Amos Andrew Garner. He has graduated from college and is now a computer programmer in Oak Ridge Tennessee. Deven completed High School in Sevier County and joined the Navy.

Bethel and I took him to Knoxville to the Crown Motel room-514 in Knoxville Tennessee, phone 522-2600 and turned him over to the Navy. A sad, sad day. December the 15th 2008 Deven reported for duty U.S. Navy, Great Lakes Illinois where he completed U.S. Navy basic training at recruit training command Great Lakes Illinios. Deven completed a variety of training which included classroom study and practical instruction on Navy customs, first aid, firefighting, water safety and emphasis on physical fitness. These exercises give recruits the skills and confidence they need to succeed in the warrior attributes of sacrifice, dedication, teamwork and endurance in each recruit and the core value of honor, courage and commitment designed to take into account what it means to be a sailor.

James, our son, took Bethel and I to Deven's graduation "Great Lakes Illinois." Deven was sent to Little River in

Virginia for a period of time then back to Great Lakes for schooling then back to Virginia. October 9, 2011 he was flown to Rome, from there to France, on to Spain, back to Virginia, then back to Great Lakes where he graduated from welding school, then back to Little River Virginia. While in Virginia he met and married Jordan Madenis. Jordan had a daughter from a previous marriage, Alexandra "Allie" who we all love. Deven and Jordan now have a son. Zackary Mark Christianer, born August 4, 2013 on a Sunday, Chesapeake, Virginia. Deven has always been like a son to Bethel and I. He spoke at Bethel's funeral. I am including a copy of it and a picture of Deven and a picture of Caylors Chapel Baptist Church in Townsend. Deven always loved this church.

Caylors Chapel Missionary Baptist Church

A sailor never abandonees his watch, He would rather die than abandonee his watch.
I don't believe my grandfather's watch ended, when he took the uniform off.
He continued to help the sick, lost and the needy through his life either by his Actions or his word in the church and out. I am proud tc
say he is my mentor and hero. All of these awards and accomplishments pined to my chest are because of the core values that he
taught me. I think this poem sums up his dedication to bettering his community and everyone in it no matter the cost.

FOR MANNY YEARS
THIS SAILOR STOOD THE WATCH

WHILE SOME OF US WERE IN OUR BEADS AT NIGHT
THIS SAILOR STOOD THE WATCH

WHILE SOME OF US WERE IN SCHOOL
THIS SAILOR STOOD THE WATCH

YES... EVEN BEFORE MOST OF US WERE BORN INTO THIS WORLD
THIS SAILOR STOOD THE WATCH

IN THOSE YEARS WHEN THE STORM CLOUDS OF WAR, WERE SEEN BREWING ON THE HORIZON
THIS SAILOR STOOD THE WATCH

MANNY TIMES HE WOULD CAST AN EYE ASHORE AND SEE HIS FAMILY STANDING THERE
NEEDING HIS GUIDANCE AND SUPPORT
NEEDING THAT HAND TO HOLD DURING THOSE HARD TIMES
BUT HE STILL STOOD THE WATCH

HE STOOD THE WATCH SO THAT WE OUR FAMILIES AND OUR FELLOW COUNTRYMEN
COULD SLEEP SOUNDLY IN SAFETY EACH AND EVERY NIGHT
KNOWING THAT A SAILOR STOOD THE WATCH

TODAY I AM HERE TO SAY
SHIPMATE YOU STAND RELIEVED

Jennifer Louise Crisp

Born June 3, 1969. Died January 31, 2008. Age 38.

Our first grandchild who we loved and raised, we loved her like she was our own. She was mistreated when she was young and never could overcome it. Bethel and I done the best we could but worried whether we had ever been good enough, only the good Lord knows.

Jennifer got cancer and died, she is buried in Mountain View Baptist Church cemetery where I will be buried between her and my husband Bethel. This is a letter she wrote to Bethel and I, Christmas 1995.

"To my Granny and Paw Christmas 1995. In this season of giving, when I stop to think on all the wonderful things in my life, the gift of your love is one of the most special. You both have given it to me freely all my life.

I remember scenes from my childhood, a little girl about to run away and Granny walking and talking to me, reminding me of all the special things we shared. Her bedtime stories, Paw and I watching Saturday morning cartoons and laughing at Roadrunner and Coyote and watching Granny in the kitchen.

I remember the afternoon I looked out the window and saw Paw with my very own pony. Paw you took the time to teach me to ride and in that, you gave me the freedom that only comes from riding a horse.

Granny you taught me to be a woman and just what that means. Times have passed and I have grown, things have changed but maybe not that much. The two of you still teach me things and I may not do as you suggest, but I don't forget what you say.

Though we have our differences and we still argue over some things, the two of you remains the single most positive influence in my life.

 Paw, you told me you didn't have an effect on my life, you taught me to think and to ask why and not just accept without questioning. You taught me how to make my voice heard.

Granny, you taught me that sometimes it is best to keep my mouth shut and and wait. I love both of you more than I can say. I live with decisions I made a few years ago. I may never have explained why I did what I did, it is like this, I couldn't give my children the kind of life they deserved. I will always love them very much, I just couldn't give them the things you gave me. I didn't know how. I live with the pain of loss every day and I have come to accept it.

 Now I am trying to go on, please forgive me if I seem to be distant at times. It is not easy. The two of you have stood by me and helped me through this and you have all my life. "Thank you!"

With all my heart, Jennifer Crisp.

Jennifer's poem

Though we may often fail To share our feelings
We hope the ones we love will somehow know
And that's why there are times
Meant for revealing the love we feel
But may not always show.
Merry Christmas to Granny and Paw
From Jennifer.

Our great grandson Deven Christianer

A great grandson who was more than a grandson. Before he was born my husband Bethel bought a trailer, had it set up on 2070 Goose Gap Road. His mom and dad, Jennifer and Mark moved in a few days before he was born. We lived up the hill from them so we could babysit often. As soon as he could talk he would say 'Up the hill." Bethel had retired. He spent a lot of time with us. At night he wanted to go to bed early so we could roll the windows out and listen to the night sounds.

We got him a Beagle dog 'Lady." She was a good dog and lived for years. We made a mistake and had her spayed and Deven cried and cried, he said is there any way you can undo what you have done? But of course we could not. We tried to make up for that by getting him a cat 'Sassy." We let her have kittens for three or four years "two litters per year." We were overcrowded with cats. He finally let us have her spayed. Sassy was a good cat, she lived for years.

Deven liked to go on trips with us. He liked to work in the garden and ride his four wheeler and go to church with us, especially Catons Chapel. He loved his Sunday school teacher, Delbert Kilbey. He fit into our plans real well. He grew up and joined the U.S. Navy 'we really missed him bad."

He met and fell in love with a girl who lived in Virginia near the Navy base, Jordan Madenis who had a little girl by a previous marriage "Little Allie." We all fell in love with her. A few years passed and they had a baby boy, Zackary. Of course we all loved him, our only great, great grandson. I always wished we lived close so I could spend time with them, but we can't have everything we want. God knows best. Maybe someday over on Heaven's shining shore.

I shall not pass through this world but once. Any good that I can do, or kindness that I can show to any human being let me do it now, for I shall not pass this way again.

My great grandson Deven Christianer's first public speech at Mountain View Missionary Baptist Church age 11 or 12. Good Morning:

The subject of our lesson today is "Finding my place in God's plan."

Key verse is: Genesis 45:7.

"And God sent me before you to preserve and save your lives by a great deliverance. To a member of the congregation (Please lead us in prayer).

Our focal passage is Genesis 45:25, 28. Please stand.

25."And they went up out of Egypt, and came into the land of Canaan unto Jacob their father. 26. And told him, saying, Joseph is yet alive, and he is governor over all the land of Egypt. And Jacob's heart fainted for he believed them not. 27. And they told him all the words of Joseph which he had said unto them, and when he saw the wagons which Joseph had sent to carry him,

The spirit of Jacob their father revived. 28. And Israel said, it is enough: Joseph my son is yet alive. I will go and see him before I die."

Do we have any birthdays or wedding anniversaries? The little children will now come to sing. You are now dismissed to your classes.

News Flash

(My namesake, Ellender Lovena Clinton Helton. Her brother, Elven "Derby" Clinton married Myrtle. They had two daughters, Audrey and Minnie. Minnie Clinton never married, died in her early 20s. Audrey had the first triplets ever registered in Sevier County).

Little Allie and Zack

My step Great Great
Granddaughter Little
Allie

Our great, great grandchild Zackary Mark Christianer
Born August 4, 2013 Chesapeake, Virginia. Weight 9lb 3oz.

To Deven and Jordan and little sister Allie "Who we all love."

Zack's father, Deven was in the U.S. Navy. Bethel only got to see Zack two times. If Bethel had been well enough we would have gone to visit and spend some time with them. The last time Bethel saw Zack, he was struggling to stay on his feet so he laid down most of the time. When Deven and his family came in he carried Zack over and laid him down with Bethel. For a two year old to be close to someone he only saw once before, he paused awhile then snuggled up like he had found the place he belonged. That gave Bethel great joy, even though Zack was so young. He brought lasting joy and contentment to a Great Grandpa.

Time went on and Bethel passed away. I would call now and then and talk to Allie. She was so sweet and always ready to talk. One time I talked to Deven awhile and he said do you want to talk to Zack? I said yes. So he put Zack on the phone and he said "Granny I love you." Deven said where did that come from? Zack's other grandparents had been to visit them and tried and tried to get Zack to say he loved them but he would not. He had that bottled up in his little mind and when he heard my voice, just let it out. I needed that. It was such a blessing to me. Little Allie is such a good child, I wish they lived close so I could baby sit and they could spend the night. I could read to them and they could go to church with me, we can't have everything we want. We just have to be thankful that things are as well as they are. God is love.

Our only Grandson Justin Ernest Crisp

Born June 22, 1989 on a Tuesday.
Named after his dad and Grandpa Ernest Justus
I always said he was born with a pencil in his hand. He never took time to be a baby, right away he would sit by the telephone with a paper and pencil ready to take notes. He would dress early in the morning in pampers, he called them "Big Boys" and his Grandpa Crisp's tie and dress hat.
He wanted to play the piano real young. His mother talked to one of their friends who gave piano lessons, and she was willing to give it a try. They tried to figure out how his feet could touch the pedals. After a few lessons Justin was playing. He was always interested in sacred music, no rock and roll or pop.
He always looked out for his little sister Olivia, and always put her first. He also was lucky to have his aunt Sheila Smith for his kindergarten teacher. When Justin was a junior at Seymour High School he spent a day in court participating in a "mock trial." Real judges oversaw the cases including Rex Henry Ogle, Dwayne Sloan and Jeff Rader. Local attorneys critiqued and scored the students. The write up in the paper said Crisp sounded like a seasoned attorney. While they waited the judges decision, Justin refused to speculate on the outcome "It's not over until it's over" he said. For the record, the attorneys scored the case in favor of the Seymour team. Attorney Gary Shin commented, "If you do become a lawyer, don't go up against me. I don't want to be creamed in the courtroom by you."

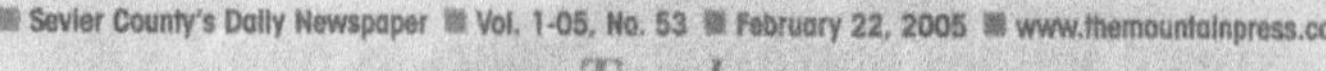

'Handwriting expert' Alex Barr explains her analysis to mock attorney Justin Crisp as his 'co-counsels' Brandon Rose, left, and Katie Thomas look observe the examination. The Seymour High School students were part of a Mock Trial competition held Monday at the Sevier County Courthouse.

Students try their best at mock trial

By BRIAN GRAVES
Staff Writer

SEVIERVILLE — Nashville singer star Carey Edward was tried in court here Monday for the murder of her manager, Jerry Cavett — sort of.

Actually, the case was tried several times over by students from Seymour, Jefferson County and Maryville high schools during a mock trial competition sponsored by the Tennessee Bar Association's (TBA) Young Lawyers Division.

The full day in court was handled much like a round-robin tournament where each team played prosecution and defense against the other.

Not only were the lawyers scored, the witnesses were also observed and judged on separating the three teams when the finals scores were tallied.

The Seymour High School team came out on top and will now travel to the state championship on March 18 and 19.

They will be using the same case that was heard Monday, which was chosen for the competition by the TBA on the merits of having equal evidence on both sides.

"There are two goals to this competition," said Seymour team coach Charles Ogle. "Students who are interested in the law can get in here and see how the courtroom feels and the justice system operates."

Ogle said the other goal is to help students with speaking skills that are important in separating the three teams when the finals scores were tallied.

All of the participants were professionally dressed, even down to the briefcases one would normally see lawyers carry into the court room.

Each side went through all of the motions of a real trial such as submitting exhibits and making objections.

"It does feel real when you are up there," said Seymour mock attorney Brandon Rose. "You do sort of get into what you are doing."

Seymour mock attorney Katie Thomas noted there is a lot of work that goes into the case they present.

"We have been working on this case for three months," she said.

Students are given only the official court charges and copies of witness depositions.

"All of the students are academically sound and involved in a lot of other activities," Ogle said. "This just takes a lot of time and real commitment."

"These students are now in high school learning rules of law I went to law school to learn," noted Mike Sayne who helps coach the Seymour team.

Area attorneys worked as jurors and judges, both figuratively and literally.

The skills of the mock attorneys made local attorney Gary Shin comment to the students, "If any of you do become lawyers, don't go up against me. You guys are that good. I don't want to get creamed in the courtroom by you."

Shin may eat his words someday when Seymour

Justin graduated from Seymour High School with honors and went on to the University of Tennessee where he graduated with honors, then on to Yale Divinity School where he graduated with honors.

Justin and Jewelle Bickel married May 21, 2016. He is now The Reverend Justin E. Crisp, Doctoral Student in Religious Studies, Yale University and Priest Associate, St. Mark's Episcopal Church, New Canaan, CT.

Olivia Jean Crisp

Born December 26, 1991.

Olivia Jean Crisp is our second granddaughter, named after both of her grandmothers Olivia Crisp and Ima Jean Justus. She was a healthy child, always easy to take care of. She was also lucky to have her aunt Sheila Smith to be her kindergarten teacher. She was eager to learn and not let her brother Justin get ahead of her.

She was always interested in animals. I think her favorite was lamb or sheep. She always said when she grew up and had her own place she wanted to have a few lamb or sheep in her backyard. When she was young she took riding lessons, she had her own pony, she still has her pony, plus two riding horses.

At an early age she saw a television commercial about "Locks of Love" giving her the idea of donating her own hair to children who had lost their hair due to medical conditions. When in the sixth grade she told her mother, "I am ready." Her mother said, "are you sure?" She said "yes, I have looked inside myself and I am ready."

Olivia and her mother went to Metropolis Hair Fashion in Knoxville, they worked and braided her hair and took a total of sixteen inches off. It felt like ten pounds were lifted off her head. Olivia continued to let her hair grow long until she was in "Vet School" and started putting animals to sleep and operating on them.

The SEYMOUR HERALD

"See more in the Seymour Herald"

AN INDEPENDENT NEWSPAPER SERVING THE 30,000 SEYMOUR AREA RESIDENTS

50 CENTS | **WEDNESDAY, DECEMBER 17 - TUESDAY, DECEMBER 23, 2003**

Love is a lock

Girl gives part of herself to help others

By Michele Karl

For sixth grader Olivia Crisp who turns twelve the end of December there was no question what she had planned with the mountain of hair that trailed down her head. "I know when I was three years old I was going to cut it off and give it to 'Locks for Love,'" stated the Seymour local. A student at Seymour Middle School, Crisp had seen a television commercial about 'Locks for Love,' giving her the idea of donating her own hair for the cause.

Based in Lake Worth, Florida, 'Locks for Love' is a non-profit organization that provides hairpieces to financially disadvantaged children under age 18 suffering from long-term medical hair loss. They meet a unique need for children by using donated hair to create the highest quality hair prosthetics.

Most of the children helped by Locks of Love have lost their hair due to a medical condition called alopecia areata, which has no known cause or cure. It is a highly unpredictable, autoimmune skin disease resulting in the loss of hair on the scalp and elsewhere on the body.

The hair is also used for cancer patients who have lost their hair due to radiation treatments. The prostheses (replacement hair) they provide help to restore the children's self-esteem and their confidence, enabling them to face the world and their peers with more ease.

"When I was three I decided I wanted to donate my hair to 'Locks for Love' for cancer victims, I had heard something on TV about it and at the time my hair was to my waist. When I had it cut it had grown to the top of my legs. At the time, it took me ten minutes every time I combed it," stated Crisp.

"One day she came up and said, 'I'm ready to do it,'" stated Olivia's mom Sherry Crisp. According to Olivia, "Last year I decided it was time to do it. I thought about it and looked inside myself and said lets do it. My mom asked if I was sure I wanted to do it then and I told her yes. I went to Metropolis Hair Fashions in Knoxville and went in and one lady washed my hair. Then another lady braided it and cut it off. They took fourteen inches off. It felt like ten pounds were lifted off my head. Then they cut off another two inches to get it evened up, for a total of 16 inches."

Please See Love pg A3

Olivia Crisp donated her lovely hair to less-fortunate children with the 'Locks for Love' program.

Newspaper clipping from the Seymour Herald "Love is a Lock."

One day she came with her dad up to see me. I looked out and thought, who is that with Joe? At first, I thought it was her mom Sherry. Then I saw it was Olivia. I said Olivia, how could you? She said Granny, what I do is more important than how I look and I knew she was right. It took time to wash and put her hair up out of the way. She said I can shower and wash my hair and shake my head and dry off and I'm ready to go.

Olivia graduated from Seymour High School with honors, with a scholarship to U.T. She later graduated from U.T. with honors and a scholarship to Veterinary Medicine at U.T. On June 7, 2014, she married William Lakatosh and will graduate in May 2018 a Doctor of Veterinary Medicine.

Her Valedictorian speech from high school is on the next page.

This Part's Over

By Joe Karl

Monday evening the Seymour Class of 2010 graduated at the Thompson Bolling Area in front of an anxious and excited audience.

My wife, my daughter and I were there to see our son's graduation ceremony as well as the rest of Seymour High Seniors beginning new lives.

The 2010 Valedictorians, Lindsay Boling, Tia Collier, Olivia Crisp, Cara Monghi, Juliet Sutphin, Andrew Turner, and D. J. Young all gave wonderful speeches. There was one that hit home to many that relates to high school life and adult life as well. That speech was by Olivia Crisp and it is copied below;

Hi guys! I'm Olivia, OCD Choir Kid and resident Harry Potter Dork. I know I will never be "normal," and you know what? I'm alright with that. When you think about it, we all seem to have these labels. We all belong to certain groups and we stay separated. It's the way the world of high school works.

But why should it be this way? We find people that we have a few things in common with and act as though everyone else in the school is just a prop on the sideline of our lives. What we forget is that these props are people too.

They have the same insecurities and emotions and dreams and secrets as us. But we chose to ignore the people outside our direct circle because it's easier that way. While we take stands on Ugg boots and sports teams, we ignore the actual people that are right in front of our faces.

In light of us being modern here, let's revamp an old Bible verse. There is neither black or white or Hispanic, jock or geek, drug addict or goodie-two-shoes, for we are all one in Christ Jesus.

Seriously, my aunt got it right when she said all we ever needed to know we learned in kindergarten- things long forgotten like how to share and If You Can't Say Anything Nice Don't Say Anything At All.

As soon to be upstanding members of society (hopefully) we have to remember that behind every reputation, good or bad, is a living, breathing, feeling person who really needs a second chance. So why don't we take our reputation and turn it into something that's actually worth something?

What if people remembered us not for how smart or strong we were, but for how we were there for them at a time when no one else cared?

What if we quit taking the easy road of letting the Props deal with their own problems, and have some compassion for our fellow humans, regardless of label? After all, Anybody can be a Somebody in the world if they take the time to care... even a Harry Potter dork.

Congratulations to all the graduating students, the faculty and the proud parents for this has been a big achievement. Think about it – 12 long years – and now it seems to have passed in a

Olivia wrote this poem for her "Paw" at age 14

GRANDPA
OLIVIA CRISP

A girl in pigtails runs up to the door.
She knocks on the door and opens her arms wide.
"Grandpa I missed you so much!" She says.
"How have you been? Thanks for the kitty.
Brother's ran off, but mine stayed with me.
I got new shoes see Grandpa?"
But girls grow up;
Pigtails are traded for nail polish and braids.

Hey, Grandpa. Are you up for a walk?
Can I see your dog Grandpa? Is she better now?
Can I go to the swing Grandpa? The bees are gone.
Would you like to go golfing with me Grandpa?
Cause you took Brother last time, and it's my turn
now.
I can't wait to clean your club heads.
And trip on the short grass after I lose.
Cause all I want is to spend time with you.
But girls grow up;
Braids are traded for music and makeup.

Hi Grandpa. Would you like to watch TV?
I brought a movie we can watch after lunch.
Can I help make breakfast Grandpa?
I like the biscuits and eggs.
Will you go to my play Grandpa?
I practiced four days a week just for you.

I hope that you can come, and Granny please come
too.
But girls grow up;
Music is traded for college.
On the phone for the first time in weeks,
"Hey, Grandpa. Are your legs better?
I'm doing great in school;
Honors Advanced Physics is very interesting.
I finally understand that verse you showed me once.
Thanks so much for helping me.
I have to go to my next class, Grandpa.
I'll talk to you next week."
But girls grow up;
And college is through and jobs appear.

Hey Grandpa, I saw a dog like yours today.
She had a bunch of healthy puppies.
And a dog was ran over today,
And it died in my arms.
I couldn't help the dog Grandpa, and I needed a hug.
That's why I came to see you.
You always were good at that.
But women keep moving,
And white dresses come up.

Hey, Grandpa. Do you like my dress?
I thought of you when I bought it.
Do you like him, Grandpa?
I want to know what you think.
He really makes me happy, Grandpa.
I love him almost as much as I love you.

He gives me flowers like Granny's,
And I think of you too.
But life continues;
And children are born.

Hey Grandpa. I have a surprise for you.
I have a little boy; his name is Joe Bethel.
I named him after the two best people in my life.
My daddy... and you Grandpa.
Isn't his nose cute? And his little feet?
Aren't you proud to be a great-grandfather?
Please be there for him.
Every game, recital, and awards day.
Please be there for him like you were for me.
But men grow old;
They aren't forever young.

A woman in black walks through the morning grass.
Hey Grandpa. Can you listen?
I had a bad night.
A litter of kittens were ran over.
They had no chance for life like I had.
They had never chased a butterfly,
Or pounced on a beetle.
Why are people so cruel Grandpa?
How can they not care for the smallest of lives?
But women don't stay young either,
They too grow older.

A woman in a rocking chair smiles broadly.
She opens her arms to her child.

"How are you Mom?" He asks.
"Growing old doesn't mean growing up, Joe.
Soon, I'll join your daddy and my parents.
And soon I'll meet my grandparents again.
I don't want a funeral, Joe; I want a party.
That will be the best day of my life, the day I go.
Because I'll join my true family."
That night the old woman flew up to the heavens.
And she died with a smile on her face.

She walked over a rainbow with animals at her heels.
She knew every one by name.
She met a litter of kittens, a dog and her puppies.
A dog that had been hit by a car licked her hand.
Strays animals great and small gathered around her.
Horses nickered and trotted up with their necks
arched.

She knew what was coming next,
As tears of joy slid down her now-smooth face.
Her husband ran to her and hugged her.
Her brother and her parents came next.
As she looked up, she saw only one thing.
I saw you Grandpa.
You were standing up straight and proud.
I walked up to you. "Hey Grandpa."

Good Advice

A seventeen year old discussed with his father about a need for a car. The father agreed but thought he needed to improve on a few things first, like his school grades, helping around the house and attending church more regularly and he thought it would be a good idea to get his hair cut.

A few months passed and the subject came up again. He said dad I have brought my grades up a little and I have been helping mom around the house and I have been attending church more regularly. His dad said how about the hair cut? The son answered, saying, dad I read in the Bible where Jesus had long hair. The father quickly replied, son if you had read a little further you would find that Jesus walked nearly everywhere he went.

Lost Dog

Three legs, blind in one eye, missing right ear, tail broken, recently castrated, answering to the name "Lucky."

Teenagers

Tired of being harassed by your stupid parents? Act now! Move out, get a job, pay your own bills while you still know everything.

Wanted A Good Woman

Must be able to clean, cook and clean fish, must have boat and motor. Send picture of boat and motor.

The School Records

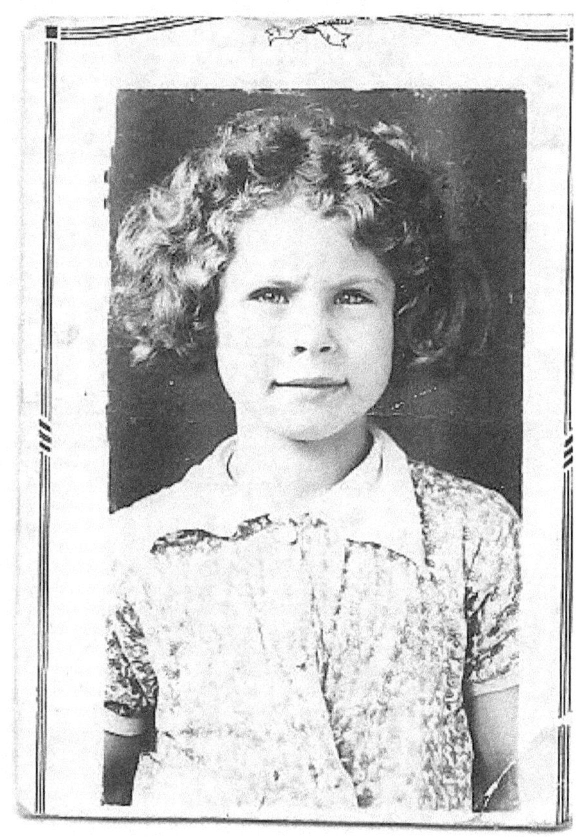

Olivia Helton Crisp

My first store bought Valentine
I received at school.

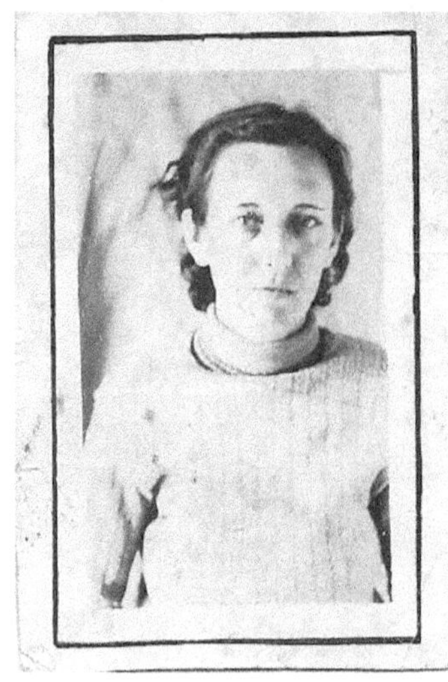

Lela King Gabble

My first teacher

SEVIER COUNTY ELEMENTARY SCHOOLS

SEVIER COUNTY, TENNESSEE

1942-19 43

REPORT OF
ATTENDANCE, SCHOLARSHIP AND PROGRESS
HEALTH CITIZENSHIP AND CHARACTER

PUPIL *Olivia Helton*

GRADE 8   SCHOOL *Bluff Mt.*

TO PARENTS

This report is not designed for the purpose of comparing the pupil with others of his class, but to inform parents as to whether or not he is making satisfactory progress.

Regularity of attendance, punctuality and faithful performace of duties are essential to the pupil to make a good school record.

System of markings:

Habits needing improvement are marked (—)

Satisfactory habits are marked (+)

EXPLANATION OF MARKINGS

E means excellent
S means satisfactory
U means unsatisfactory.

SCHOLASTIC ACHIEVEMENTS

MONTHS	1	2	3	4	5	6	7	8	9
1. Observes health rules	+	+	+	+	+	+	+	+	
2. Is polite in speech and action	+	+	+	+	+	+	+	+	
3. Is prompt in all duties	+	+	+	+	+	+	+	+	
4. Is truthful and can be trusted	+	+	+	+	+	+	+	+	
5. Makes effort to control temper	+	+	+	+	+	+	+	+	
6. Is neat and orderly	+	+	+	+	+	+	+	+	
7. Makes good use of time	+	+	+	+	+	+	+	+	
8. Depends on self	+	+	+	+	+	+	+	+	
9. Makes effort toward improvement	+	+	+	+	+	+	+	+	
10. Is a good school citizen	+	+	+	+	+	+	+	+	
Days present:						20			
Days absent:	+	+				0			
Times tardy:									
Deportment:	90	90	90	90	90	93	96	90	

Remarks:

MONTHS	1	2	3	4	5	6	7	8	9
LANGUAGE ARTS									
Reading	S	S	E	E	E	E	E	E	
Language	S	S	S	S	S	S	S	S	
Spelling	S	S	E	E	E	E	S	S	
Writing	S	S	S	S	S	S	S	S	
SOCIAL STUDIES									
History	S	S	S	S	S	S	S	S	
Civics	S	S	S	S	S	E	S	S	
Geography									
Forestry & Conservation									
APPRECIATION									
Art	S	S	S	S	S	E	E	E	
Music	E	E	E	E	E	E	E	E	
Library (Books read)									
Health	S	S	S	S	S	S	S	S	
Arithmetic	S	S	S	S	S	S	S	S	

REMARKS:

Parents, you are cordially invited to confer with the teacher on any matter pertaining to your child's progress and welfare.

You are respectfully requested to sign and return this card at once. Your signature simply shows that you have seen this report; it does not necessarily show approval.

1. ____
2. ____
3. ____
4. ____
5. ____
6. ____
7. ____
8. ____

This is to certify that _Olivia Helton_

is promoted

is retained in ______9th______ grade.

Teacher ____________________________________

Principal _Bonnie A. Shultz_

Co. Supt. THERON H. HODGES

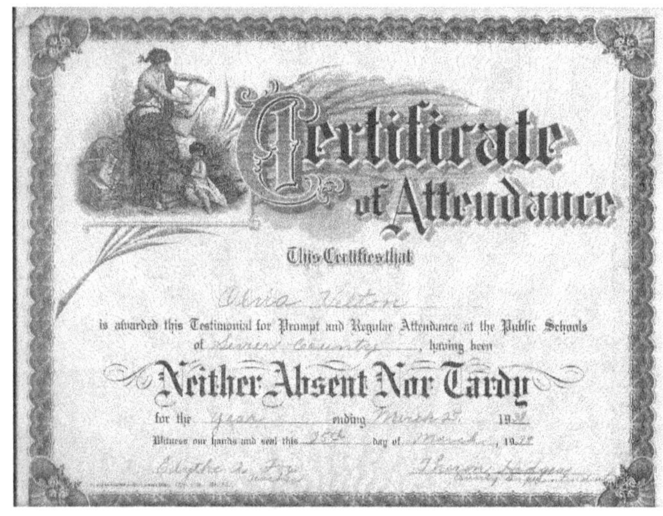

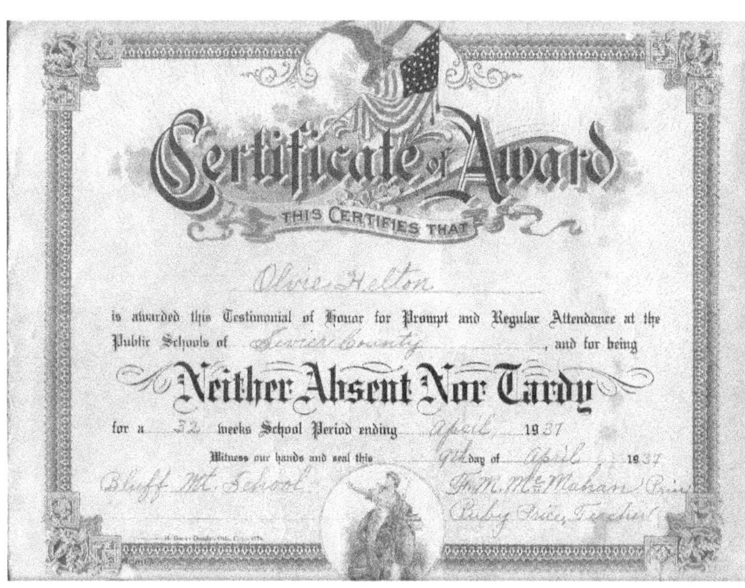

Certificate of Award
THIS CERTIFIES THAT
Olivia Helton
is awarded this Testimonial of Honor for Prompt and Regular Attendance at the
Public Schools of Sevier County, and for being
Neither Absent Nor Tardy
for a 32 weeks School Period ending April, 1937
Witness our hands and seal this 9th day of April 1937
Bluff Mt. School
F. M. McMahan, Prin.
Ruby Price, Teacher

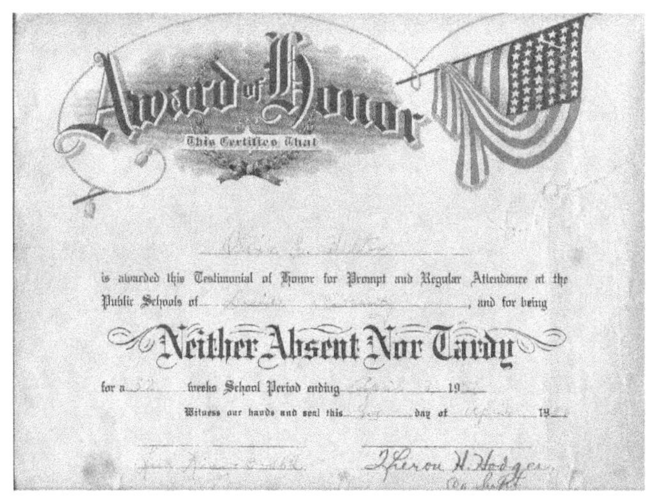

Award of Honor
This Certifies That
is awarded this Testimonial of Honor for Prompt and Regular Attendance at the
Public Schools of, and for being
Neither Absent Nor Tardy
for a weeks School Period ending 19
Witness our hands and seal this day of 19
Theron H. Hodges

TENNESSEE
PUBLIC SCHOOLS
CERTIFICATE

Whereas Olvia Helton of Bluff Mountain School
Sevier County, Tennessee, has completed the Elementary
Course of Study in the Branches required by Law to be taught in the Public Schools and
is entitled to enter the first year of any High School in the State.

Now, therefore, this Certificate is awarded by the State of Tennessee.

In testimony whereof witness our signatures.

Given at Bluff Mt. School in the County of Sevier State of Tennessee
this 2nd day of April A.D. 1942
Mrs. Bonnie A. Shulty, Principal Theron H Hodge County Superintendent of Schools
B. C. Townsend, Chairman of Board of Education R. D. Duggan, Commissioner of Education

Motar Branch School

Class members of Motar Branch School in 1924 which was located on Goose Gap Road, Route 5, Sevierville. The teachers were Edith Davenport (Mrs. Walter Ogle) and M.W. Tarwater. Mrs. Velma Ogle Ward, member of the class, is the owner of this picture.

The members are, back row from left, Marshall Gibson, Frank Breeden, Clarence Atchley, Elmer Helton, Roy Trentham, Knaffle Whaley, Louis Ogle, Bates Ward, John Huff, West McGill, Clyde Huff, Carl Ogle, unidentified, Cloun Whaley, James Shular, Hugh Andes, Jessie Helton. Second row, from left, M.W. Tarwater, teacher, Thad Ogle, Shannon Kirby, Edgar Huff, unidentified, Jobby Green, Frank Baker, Mack Helton, Herman Helton, Jimmy McGill, Beecher Kirby, Oscar Ward, Willie Mae Reagan, Carl Shular, Jack Helton, unidentified, Reva Andes, Vernon Shular, Alma Ward, Edith Davenport, teacher.

Third row, Ola Houk, Velma Ogle, Mae Huff, Erma Houk, Irene Gibson, Stella McGill, Pauline Atchley, Willie McGill, Rebecca Trentha, Ruby Whaley, Hazel Baker, Ruby Inman, Ina Helton, Cecil Andes, Gladys Shular, Bernice Benson. Fourth and fifth row, Ella Breeden, Woodruff Kirby, Clarence Helton, Robert Helton, Lecta Shular, Kate Ogle, Zora Helton, Eliza Helton, Wilburn Helton, Hansel Ogle, Betty Trentham, Raymond Reagan, unidentified, Carl Helton, Bill Helton, Claude Shular, Edna Ogle, unidentified, Adis Atchley, Ruth Houk, Kate Ogle, Etheleene Helton.

Mortar Branch School

Farther back than I can remember Mortar Branch School was just off Goose Gap Road on Mortar Branch Road. I have a picture (shown) dated 1924, five years before I was born. In the picture there are 71 or 72 children and 2 teachers beside them. M.W. Tarwater and Edith Davenport or possibly Mrs. Walter Ogle.

There are four of my siblings in that picture. The source of their water was a cistern or hand dug well. I don't know why or when the school was closed. After Mortar Branch was closed they had school at 2070 Goose Gap Road in a large one room house called the Missie House. They also had church there before Mountain View Baptist Church was built. "I remember going to church there."

Around 1934, Bluff Mountain School was built, they got their supplies from Elkmont when the Smoky Mountains became a national park and families and businesses had to relocate. So the supplies to build Bluff Mountain School came from Elkmont. It was located just a stone's throw from the old Missie House.

I was not old enough to go to school but a teacher, Lela King Gobble came out and talked to my parents and said they needed me in order to keep two teachers so I went. Lela was a real teacher. The school was a two room school, teaching grades from primer to eighth grade. There was two cloak rooms used to hold coats and caps, store books, brooms, mops and school supplies. Each room had a large heater, heated by wood or coal. Each year a truck came from the coal mines of Virginia. In each room each teacher had their table and a chair. At the front of the room there was a blackboard on the wall with plenty of chalk and erasers.

There was no running water or electricity, no indoor plumbing, there was two outside toilets, one for boy's one for girl's on the opposite side of the school. I am pretty sure the first well that was ever dug in Goose Gap was at the school. The principle rang a handbell at 8 o'clock each morning, we formed two lines, one for the little room and one for the big room. We all marched in and stood by our seats and repeated the pledge to the flag. We then were seated. The teacher read a few verses from the Bible and said a prayer "The Lord's Prayer.""

We recited the Ten Commandment and the Golden Rule. Then we were ready for our classes. We broke for recess about 10 o'clock, got a drink, used the bathrooms and played a few games then back to study until 12 o'clock, lunch time. The children who lived close like me and my siblings ran home for lunch and hoped for a baked sweet potato or corn on the cob, til we could grab it and run back to the school and play. The children who brought their lunch would usually bring a baked potato, boiled egg, corn on the cob: peanut butter was almost unheard of.

We played many games like jump rope, hopscotch, annie over, marble, jack rocks and fox and dog. We had a basketball and baseball team We was pretty good. We beat Gatlinburg in the tournament. The way we would travel was usually in the back of a truck. Between the two rooms were sliding doors which could be opened up for special events and occasions such as speaking programs, telling stories, having a spelling B. My favorite poem was "Twinkle, Twinkle Little Star." We had Christmas plays where the parents and public was invited to come. We would exchange gifts, sing Christmas Carols, sometimes have a Santa Claus. This also gave parents and teachers a chance to get acquainted. At Easter we had Easter egg hunts where they would give prizes and have a lucky egg. We had no egg dye. We used sage brush, walnut shells and crape paper. At Halloween we made jack-o-lanterns and told scary tales.

Anyway, Bluff Mountain was a good school we had good teachers, sometimes teachers stayed in the community because they had no transportation to travel.We had a teacher who stayed at our home Sunday evening through Friday morning. Once per year we walked to the top of Bluff Mountain taking our lunch stopping at the Devil's Den and the Hotel place where years ago people came from Knoxville and various places taking their vacation.

When World War II was on, they completed the bridge at Douglas Dam. The teacher took us in the back of a truck to see the great Douglas Dam, something we will never forget. When I was twelve years old our teacher Walter Ogle marched us out to Mountain View Baptist Church where they were having a revival. That's where I got saved. I was baptized in the creek with about twenty more near where Goats on the Roof is on Wears Valley Road. When I was 17 or 18 years old I was the substitute teacher for the low grades at Bluff Mountain School. I got my High School Diploma after I was married.

My Mom and Dad
William Andrew Helton and Haretta Caroline Ward Helton

My mother and dad's family:

William Andrew Helton. Born March 28, 1892. Died October 25, 1952 Age 60.
Haretta Caroline "Hattie" Ward. Born June 27, 1896. Died February 5, 1982. Age 85. Were married June 25, 1911.

Their children:
#1. Mack David. Born August 19, 1912. Died January 28, 1998. Age 85.

#2. Mary I. Zora. Born October 29, 1914. Died October 14, 1981. Age 66.

#3. Hugh Wilburn. Born March 16, 1917. Died June 10, 1997. Age 80.

#4. Eliga Andrew. Born February 25, 1919. Died October 30, 2000. Age 81.

#5. Nellie Lea. Born October 9, 1921.

#6. Callie Juanita. Born April 6, 1924.

#7. Charles Hurbert. Born September 22, 1926.

#8. Olivia Ellender. Born March 4, 1929.

#9. Reece. Born November 18, 1932. Died July 11, 2012. Age 79.

#10. Annice. Born February 16, 1935.

#11. Lynn Allen. Born July 16, 1938.

Marriages:
#1. Mack David married Hazel Cutshaw June 22, 1937.
Children:
Maxine who married Bruce Stinnett; Helen Louise who married Rev. Edward Parton (Mack and Hazel were divorced). Mack married Kathaline Johnson January 25, 1958. Kathaline died July 6, 1992. Age 70.
#2. Mary I. Zora married Frank Montgomery November 28, 1936.
Children:
Rev. David Ellis Montgomery Mary Helen Montgomery. Frank died March 19, 1943. Age 31. Zora died October 14, 1981. Age 66.
#3 Hugh Wilburn married Dorothy Irene Rule October 4, 1936.
Children:
Iva Irene and Jo Anne.
Dorothy died June 10, 1989. Jo Anne died (Date?). Wilburn died June 10, 1997. Age 80.
#4. Eliga Andrew married Myrtle Evon Hall January 8, 1946.
Children:
David, Larry, Tommy and Shirley Louise. Myrtle died October 7, 1990. Eliga died October 30, 2000. Age 81.
David Allen born December 25, 1946. Died December 10, 1990.

#5. Nellie Lea married Wilford Watson June 17, 1942.
Children:
William Homer, Carolyn Ann, Linda Lea and Jack.
Wilford died June 28, 1972. Age 48.
#6. Callie Juanita married Grady Lowe April 16, 1946.
Children:
Brenda Sue and Patricia Ann and Jerry Olin. Grady died December 1, 1967. Age 51. Jerry Olin born April 6 1942, died April 7, 1942.
Juanita's second marriage July 21, 1973 to Henry Charles (H.C.) Minton. H.C. Died June 12, 1993. Age 66.
Juanita's third marriage to James Abbott October 29, 1996. James died September 29, 2005. Age 89.
#7. Charlie Hubert married Wilma Roberts February 11, 1946.
Children:
Hubert Helton. Wilma died October 27, 1997.
#8. Olivia Ellender Helton married Bethel Chandler Crisp October 9, 1947.
Children:
James William, Howard Donald and Joe Ernest.
Bethel died June 20, 2015. Age 89
#9. Reece married Lillie Mae Suttles November 23, 1956.
Children:
Steve Reece, Debora, Karen and Judy. Reece died July 11, 2012.
#10. Annice married Charles Huskey December 4, 1953.
Children:
Peggy Lynn, Charles (Chucky) and Nickie Paul. Charles died December 23, 1992. Age 56. Annice second marriage to Jack Rogers April 21, 2001.

#11. Lynn Allen married Betty Jo Holland October 26, 1956.
Children:
Jo Anna Lynn, William Ronald Eugene and Patricia Juanita.

My Mom Haretta Caroline Ward Helton

Eliga Andrew Helton (Served in WWII)

Pitcher Claude Crisp, Struck out 26 men and caught a pop up fly for the 27th out in one game Bryson City, N.C.

Me and my little sister Annice

Cementary at Valley town in Andrews, N.C. Where Bothies Mother & Dad Brother & Sisters. plus many other relatives are berried

Charlie Helton (with a rabbit) Bluff Mountain in the background.

Yesterday's Antiques on Wears Valley Road Where my dad's family lived, on one hundred and sixty acres of land, when the "White Caps" killed my dad's dad when my dad was only 2 years old.

My mother Hattie Helton and all 11 children

Mom and Dad at home in Goose Gap

(Top) My brother Eliga who served in WWII (Bottom)
Bethel's brother James Crisp, WWII (killed in Belgium).

After my dad had been dead 15 years, my mom married
Lee Myers. He was a good step dad.

My sister Juanita and her husband Grady Lowe.

My mom, sister Zora, brother Mack and his wife Kathaline

Home of Claude and Alice Crisp. Andrews, N.C.

My Brother Lynn Allen and wife Betty Jo.

The Crisp family

Olivia and Bethel

Bethel Crisp U.S. Navy WWII

Olivia (Graduation)

Bethel and Howard at home in Detroit Mi.

Olivia and Bethel at the home of Claude and Alice Crisp
Andrews, N.C.

Mom, James and Howard at home on Goose Gap Road

Bethel and sons

Olivia and sons

Bethel and Olivia at home in Seymour

Bethel, Olivia, Bill Helton and David Montgomery
(50th wedding anniversary)

James first day at school (Bluff Mountain)

James, Howard and Joe with their donkey at Seymour.

Bethel baptizing his son James (Burnett's Creek)

Bethel baptizing his son Howard (Cold Springs Church)

Joe as a baby at Crisp Grocery Store Goose Gap Road

Bethel baptizing his son Joe (Cold Springs Baptist Church)

James and Howard caught 2

The Crisp Brothers Band

James dancing in Hawaii

Joe, Bethel and Olivia at Seymour High School
Veterans Day Program 2009

The Cowboy's Ten Commandments

(posted on the wall at Cross Trails Church in Fairlie, Texas)

(1) Just one God.
(2) Honor yer Ma & Pa.
(3) No tellin' tales or gossipin'.
(4) Git yourself to Sunday meetin'.
(5) Put nothin' before God.
(6) No foolin' around with another
   fellow's gal.
(7) No killin'.
(8) Watch yer mouth.
(9) Don't take what ain't yers.
(10) Don't be hankerin' for yer buddy's stuff.

Howard Square Dance Calling

My Sunday School Class
Lillie Ogle, Olivia Crisp, Rose Huskey, Eloise Ownby, Emma Ownby, Lucille McCarter, Grace Joslin, Ada McPherson, and Dorothy McFalls.

James and Paulette

James and Paulette Crisp

Mom & Dad

Fifty-six years ago, July 28 1948, you saw fit to bring into this world a son.

I, James William Crisp, am that son.

Thank You are words that sometime in today's society seem to have little meaning. However, I can think of no other more meaningful words to say to you than THANK YOU. Thank you for giving me the chance to live, thank you for giving me instructions, thank you for all the help you have given over the years and thank you for the confidence you have in me. You help to make July 28 Happy Birthday to me.

Howard and Carolyn Crisp

Joe and Sherry Crisp

Lynn Allen, Olivia, Wilburn, Bethel, Juanita, Nellie, Reece.

There's a place within
Our hearts where
memories abound,
Where glimpses of our
loved ones and happy
times are found...
We only have to go there
to find strength to carry
on And realize our loved
ones are never really
gone.

Eliga A. Helton
&
Juanita Rayfield
Family & Grand Children
&
Great Grand Children

For My
Dear Wife,
Olivia
on Mother's Day

You've created
something wonderful
in my life —
something beautiful...

Being with you
has given new meaning
to each day
we welcome together.
And, with you, I've found
something within
a confidence, a strength
I never knew without you.

You are my inspiration,
my reason for happiness.
You are my wife
and my joy forever.

Happy Mother's Day
with
My Love Always

I love you.

Rachel

Bethel's retirement from Rohm & Haas Feb. 28, 1986
(John Miller)

Mountain View Baptist Church Cemetery

MAY 22 2012-MAY 26 2013
NAMES OF VETERANS BURIED IN MTN. VIEW BAPTIST CHURCH CEMETERY

1. WALLACE BAKER
2. JAMES D. BOHANAN
3. ROGER LYNN BOHANAN
4. DAVID RONALD BOYKIN
5. CHARLIE CHRISTOPHER
6. JOHNNIE DWAIN DENNY
7. ELISHA FLOYD
8. TERANCE FLOYD
9. RICHARD GIBSON
10. HUGH GREEN
11. CHARLES WALTER HAYES
12. JOHN DAVID HAYES
13. JOHN RUSSELL HAYES
14. ARTHUR HELTON
15. CLYDE HELTON
16. OSCAR HELTON
17. REECE HELTON
18. BILL HUFF
19. JIM HUSKEY
20. HENRY JUSTUS
21. DOT KING
22. OTHA REX KING
23. ROBERT LACY
24. WILLIAM M. LANE
25. WILLIAM VIRGIL LATHAM
26. DONALD LINDSEY
27. CLOUMBUS LOWE
28. GRADY LOWE
29. CARL H. MCCARTER

30. REAFORD MCCARTER
31. ELMER MCPHERSON
32. PAUL MCPHERSON
33. HENRY MINTON
34. BEECHER OGLE
35. CARMIE OGLE
36. JAMES WILFORD OGLE
37. RALPH PARLON OGLE
38. PARLON RICHARD OGLE
39. KENNETH DOYLE OWNBY
40. DAVID PARTON
41. CARL COLLINS PATE
42. DEWEY PRICE
43. EARL PRICE
44. FAIN TROTTER PRICE
45. WALTER RAMSEY
46. CHARLIE RAYFIELD
47. TRES RAYFIELD
48. VIRGIL RAYFIELD
49. FRED BOYD REVELS
50. LUTHER UNDERWOOD
51. WILLIAM UNDERWOOD
52. JAMES L. WARD
53. OSCAR D. WARD
54. ROGER WARD
55. WILFORD WATSON
56. DEWEY BUD WHALEY
57. LUKE WHALEY
58. DAVID CLYDE WILLIAMS
59. William Homer WATSON
60. BeThel C. Crisp

These are the names of veterans buried in the Mountain View
Baptist Church cemetery Goose Gap Road

Our First Grandchild

Jennifer Louise Crisp born June 3, 1969, married Mark Christianer had two sons: Deven Caleb born November 3, 1989 (Friday).Amos Andrew, Chase Wesley born January 3, 1992 (Friday). Jennifer died January 31, 2008. Age 38. Zakary Mark Christianer born August 4, 2013 (Sunday). Deven caleb Christianer married Jordan Madinis and little Allie March 2011. Zackary was born August 4, (Monday) 2013.

Jennifer's first day of school
(Prospect School Blount Co.)

Jennifer & her dog at home in Seymour

Jennifer's wedding at Mountain View Church

Jennifer and her Grandpa Bethel

Jennifer and her dad Howard Crisp

Petty Officer Deven Christianer

Deven Christianer and step-daughter (Little Allie)

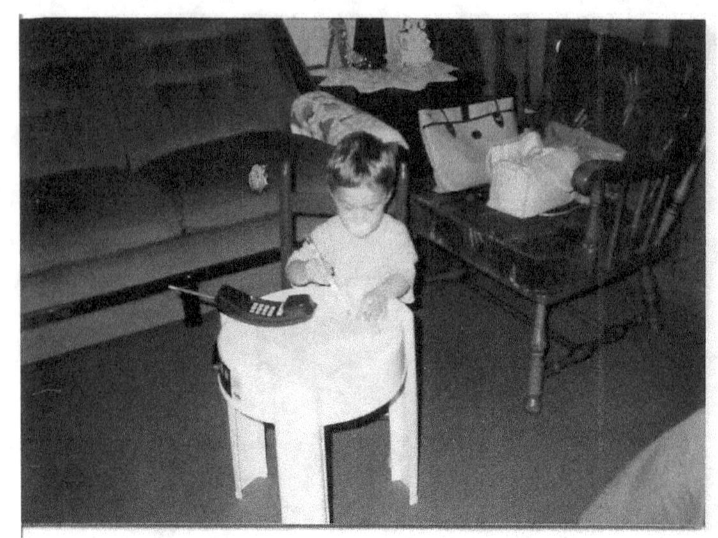

Justin Crisp

Olivia and Justin

Deven Christianer

Amos Andrew Garner (Grad. Headstart 1998)

Great Grandson Amos Andrew Garner

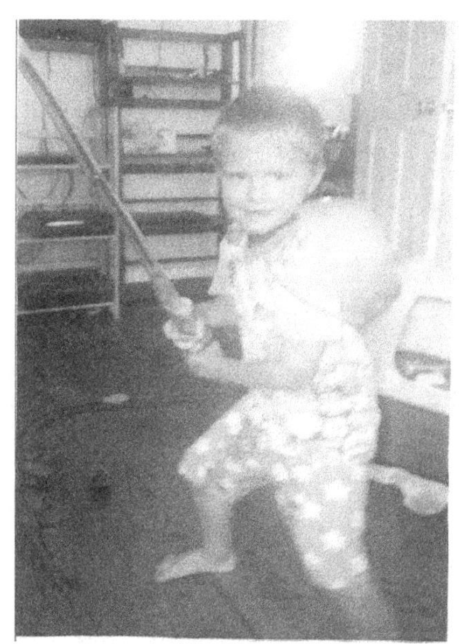

Zackary

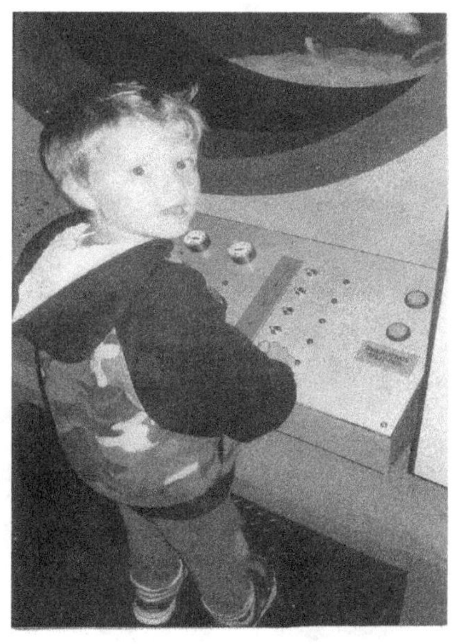

Zackary

Deven and Jordan's Wedding, Manteo, NC

Olivia and William's Wedding, Knoxville, TN

Justin and Jewelle's Wedding, New Canaan, CT

From Around Sevier County
Photos and Newspaper Clippings
(Mountain Press)

Lucy Crisp at Dolly's statue on the Courthouse lawn in
Sevierville, TN.

View of Bluff Mountain and our home from the opposite side of Goose Gap Road. Below is Bluff Mountain on fire

Curt Habraken/The Mountain Press

Mike and Cindy Morris felt called to serve as house parents at The Home, where they've been doing just that for the past two years.

First Children's Home Orphanage

House parents giving children a chance

Children with the Church of God Orphanage in Cleveland, Tenn., pose for a photo in this undated photo. The orphanage eventually moved from Cleveland to Sevier County and is now known as The Home.

90 YEARS OF HOPE AND HEALING

Submitted

The orphanage grew over the years to accept more children in need of a home. Beginning in one small frame house, two more houses were added before a larger facility was built in Cleveland on 119 acres to house several hundred children.

Submitted

The Home made its move to Sevierville in 1949, occupying the building that used to serve as the Church of God Bible Training School.

Submitted

A resident of The Home climbs the tower as part of the Certified Ropes Course, which helps youth develop self-esteem, improve confidence and learn to trust themselves.

Home on the range

Local family tries their hand at raising buffalo

By JASON DAVIS
Sports Editor

Motorists on Seymour's Porterfield Gap Road could be in for quite a surprise as the approach the intersection with East Union Valley.

Standing in the field at the adjacent Ingle Farms, they're likely to see an animal that hasn't roamed the wilds of Tennessee for nearly 200 years.

Four American bison, more commonly referred to as buffalo, reside on Edward Ingle's farm and can often be seen easily from the road.

"(People) stop all the time, bring their kids down here (to see the bison)," Ingle said. "And (the buffalo) will just stand there and eat."

Ingle took up the hobby of raising bison at the insistence of his wife, Angie.

"We were going to raise some for meat, and we saw some in the paper," he said.

He purchased the three heifers and bull nearly a year and a half ago.

"The heifers came from over here on Straw Plains," Ingle said, "He had 10 cows and a bull, and he just raises them and sells the calves."

Ingle's bison aren't old enough to breed yet, but in another year he hopes they start producing some calves, from which he'll eventually have a steady supply of meat.

"They say the meat's a lot better, healthier, than beef is," Ingle said.

According to the National Bison Association (NBA), it is.

"Comparisons to other meat sources have also shown that Bison has a greater concentration of iron as well as some of the essential fatty acids necessary for human well being," the association said on its website.

"Research ... at North Dakota State University has shown that the meat from bison is a highly nutrient dense food because of the proportion of protein, fat, mineral, and fatty acids," the association continued.

About a million pounds of bison meat, which is said to have a sweeter, richer flavor than beef, is consumed yearly by American consumers, according to the USDA.

As far as care goes, Ingle said there's not much difference between raising bison and regular cattle.

"Really they're no harder to take care of than cattle," Ingle, who also has around 100 cows and several walking horses, said.

In fact, in some ways they could actually be lower-maintenance, according to the National Bison Association.

According to the NBA, bison require no artificial shelter, they are extremely disease resistant and they calve without outside assistance while thriving on most American landscapes.

One major difference between the two species is that bison are not domesticated animals.

No special permits are required to own bison, but extra care should be

See BUFFALO, Page C2

The Ingle farm in Seymour is home to four American bison, or buffalo, being raised to produce more calves for meat.

Edward Ingle stands beside the enclosed pasture where his buffalo roam, just off Porterfield Gap road in Seymour. He's owned the four young buffaloes since they were six months old.

"

Reception held for 'A Beautiful View'

The King Family Library held this in honor of Marion Oats and her book about the local history of Bluff Mountain.

Friends and acquaintances of Marian Oates at the reception in honor of her book of memories and history of Bluff Mountain.

The Oat's family was one of the first to build and own property way up on Bluff Mountain

READING, 'RITING & 'RITHMATIC

Jason Davis/The Mountain Press

Sam Lyle, one of the heirs of the Mack Hammer property where the school sits, walks from the porch as repairs were being made on Thursday.

Jason Davis/The Mountain Press

The bell tower of Island View School had been sagging until recent repairs righted its stance. A bell rung in the tower Thursday for the first time in over 50 years, Sam Lyle estimated.

Tom McCarter/The Mountain Press

Steve Sipos works inside the school, where old blackboards still hang on the walls and other signs of its former days are also evident.

The Flood in Sevierville

Water, Water, Everywhere

Sequence of photos shows water's rapid rise

LOVE ADDITION 9:15 a.m. By this time most residents had been evacuated and were waiting out the coming of the flood crest on higher ground. People were talking quietly in groups hoping for the best—fearing the worst.

SAME SPOT 11:00 a.m. Mailbox in first picture almost under. Water is now in all houses in this area. Most people report around three inches more water than they had in the March 1963 flood.

Gone with the tide

SMALL HOUSE that sat on this spot on old Knox Highway was carried completely away Friday by flood waters. The residence of Burly Floyd, witnesses said the house simply moved off into the current and soon disappeared. Concret block pillars can be seen overturned. Furniture and belongings have not been found

PITTMAN CENTER ELEMENTARY SCHOOL, first through sixth grade building at left and gymnasium seem to be floating as creeks spread over the valley isolating the school buildings. Pupils were not in school.

PFC. Clyde EHelton
Born Aug. 16-1923
Killed in World War ll in France Nov-25-1944
He was the Son of Johnny and Martha Helton
He had eight brothers, Boyd, Odis, Hobert, Ernest,
Carl, Bill, Arthur, Oscar and Elmer.
Four sisters Alma White, Margie Allen,
Lillian Loveday and Mary Bell Goosie.
His body was brought back to the United States
And received at Atchleys Funeral Home
Sept 15-1948
He is buried in Mt. View Baptist Cemetery

Dupont Springs Hotel once graced Bluff Mountain

Guests gather for a picture in front of Dupont Springs Hotel in 1909.

Dupont Springs Hotel opened in 1901 and closed in 1916.

The Flora Swann owned by the Knox, Sevier and Jefferson Steamboat Company.

Photo courtesy of Bob Newman

The Pines was Sevierville's first movie theater

The Pines Theater when "Made for Each Other," starring Carole Lombard was showing. The film came out in 1939.

Submitted

The interior of the Pines Theatre, with a seating capacity of over 700.

Railroad service began in Sevier County in 1910

Sevierville's first KS&E agent T.J. Stafford (right) and E.G. McAfee stand in front of the first permanent railroad depot in Sevierville in 1910

Dan Davenport played his banjo for square dances at Henderson Springs Resort.

Several guests are pictured standing on the porches of the second Henderson Springs Hotel which was built in 1898.

Ruby Henderson Sims daughter of hotel manager

Submitted

Alf Newman in front of Newman's Café in 1988.

Alf Newman standing beside one of his cabs in 1947.

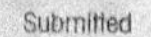
Submitted

The interior of Newman's Café in 1956.

Submitted

Central Hotel fixture in Sevierville many years

Submitted

The first Central Hotel building was a two-story clapboard structure.

Joseph E. Bowers operated the Central Hotel from 1902 until his death in 1912.

The New Central Hotel was built in 1924 and dismantled in 1968.

Douglas Dam during autumn.

Construction of temporary dike and river arr
cofferdam. Cofferdams were built across the riv
allow enclosed area to be pumped out thereby (
ing a dry work area

River rechanneled to help prevent flooding

Corner of Bruce Street and Court Avenue on Jan. 31, 1957. Curiously, the street sign is turned incorrectly.

Court Avenue at the corner of Commerce Street and Court Avenue on March 12, 1963.

Red's Cafe was a fixture in downtown Sevierville

Red Clevenger standing in front of the last Red's Cafe, located on Court Avenue.

Submitted

Virginia Trotter and Erskine Stafford were married on Dec. 22, 1941, and died in a car accident en route to their honeymoon.

Virginia Trotter was teaching third grade at Sevierville Elementary School when she married Erskine Stafford.

Sevier's Blowing Cave Mill was built in 1880

Located near the intersection of Blowing Cave Road and Byrd's Cross Road, Blowing Cave Mill (above) was built by Early Brothers in 1880. In 1941, a steel water wheel (right) replaced the original wooden wheel at Blowing Cave Mill Blowing Cave Mill.

Harrisburg bridge has rich history in county

The Harrisburg Covered Bridge today.

Submitted

The Harrisburg Covered Bridge as it stood before its 1976 renovation.

Submitted

Baptist Assoc. elects officers

The 87th session of the Sevier County Baptist Association came to a close Wednesday, October 18, at 2:45 p.m.

General officers elected in that meeting, the last of five sessions beginning Monday night, October 16, were: Bethel Crisp, moderator; Earl Lane, vice-moderator; Carl Ownby, treasurer; and Miss Maxine Hodge, clerk.

Action was taken to accept the proposal of the Executive Committee to have a county-wide crusade in July of 1973. The body also voted to have a booth at the Sevier County Fair next year.

A climactic moment was the burning of a note on the Associational Missionary home, paid for by the Sevier Baptist Association. The note-burning took place at the Tuesday evening session with the moderator, Bethel Crisp, holding the plate while Clyde Ownby and Carl Ownby assisted.

Members of the building committee and the Board of Trustees, past and present, were asked to take part in the note-burning ceremony.

According to a digest of information from all Sevier County churches, there are 61 Southern Baptist churches in Sevier County. Those churches reported 397 baptisms through the year, 322 additions by letter, making a total membership in all churches of 14,257.

First Baptist Church of Sevierville, with a membership of 1290 is largest. Pigeon Forge First Baptist is second in size with an 862 membership and Gatlinburg First Baptist is third with 561 members.

Bethel Crisp catches the ashes of a burning note, denoting the last payment on the home for Sevier County Baptist Associational Missionary. Assisting in the note-burning are Clyde Ownby, left, and Carl Ownby

Bethel Crisp, Moderator of Sevier County Baptist Association, burns the note denoting the last payment on the home for the Sevier County Missionary Baptist Association. Assisting in the note burning are Clyde Ownby and Carl Ownby

The old Public Square on Main Street in Sevierville was the hub of activity for more than a century.

The circular area of the Public Square is pictured during its construction in 1924. The building under construction is the second Central Hotel.

Store prices from the early days
Of 1972

'Beecher' made name in music

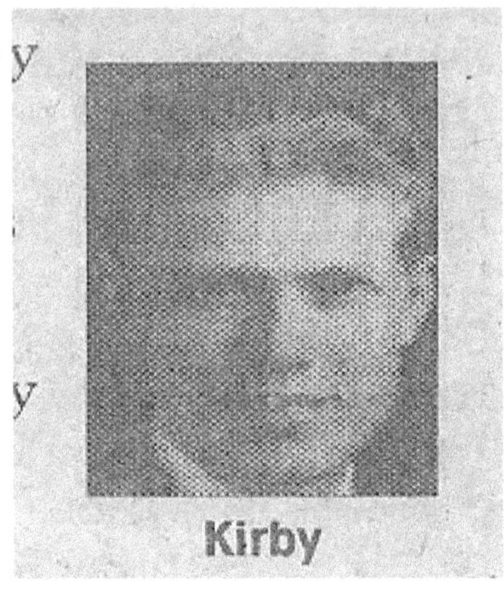

Kirby

Roy Acuff and Beecher Kirby performing on the Grand Ole Opry stage.

Beecher Kirby with two of his favorite instruments.

Rindy Bailey known for her rambling

Rindy Bailey was a legend- ary homeless figure in the last half of the 1800s around the Kodak community.

Matthews known for music

The mandolin owned by Fred Matthews was handed down to his great-nephew, Jeff Matthews.

Fred Matthews with his mother, Mary Jane Matthews.

Fred Matthews was an East Tennessee Musician and songwriter

My Hands

My hands though wrinkled and rough, are the tools I have used to embrace life. They caught my falls when as a toddler I stumbled and fell. They put clothes on my back and food in my mouth. They tied my shoelaces, clung to my mother's apron strings, toiled in the fields with my dad, created a strong bond with my children.

My mother taught me to fold them in prayer. Decorated with my wedding band that showed the world that I was married and loved someone special, they were uneasy and clumsy as I held my newborn sons.

They have been bruised and dirty as I worked to provide a comfortable home and healthy meals for my family. They wrote letters to loved ones and trembled as I stood by their graves. They have helped my children, grandchildren and great grandchildren and many older invalids who couldn't do for themselves. Yes, I am thankful for my hands. They have served me well.

Olivia Helton Crisp.

The best compliment I ever got

"The best compliment I ever got" was when I went to U.T. Hospital in Knoxville, Tennessee to visit my good friend and neighbor Cleo Davis Garner. She had cancer and was near death. Her fever was high, I asked her if I could get a pan of water and bathe her, she said if you don't care. I started bathing her, she said, "I feel like the angels have took hold of me."

I'll be home before dark
(written by Charles Wycuff)

Often in my mind I wonder to my younger days
When I roamed the hills and valleys in my childhood ways
But I could always remember mother's last remarks
She had made as I was leaving. You be home before dark.

I'll be home before the darkness falls in this weary land
I'll be resting with the ones I love on the golden strand
When the supper table has been set, before they start
I'll be safely in my Father's house, I'll be home before dark.

If the Lord delays his coming to this earth again
I may go by death to glory heavens grand domain
But there won't be any darkness there, when I shall
embark
Through the valley of the shadows
I'll be home before dark.

At Journey's End

As I come to the end of my journey, I look back to my childhood. Goose Gap, Sevierville, Tennessee, the place where I was born into a family of love, six brothers and four sisters. I could not have had a better mom and dad, two people who gave their life raising eleven children, working and planning, scrimping and saving, giving the best they had trying to prepare us for a good life. Training us to want to do the best we could, knowing how to live a useful and happy life, to know how to manage and apply ourselves to be able to face life's tragedies and to look back and to know we had done our best.

I am happy to say all the family members have been on speaking terms and ready to help each other right onto the end. I think back at the time I met Bethel "The love of my life" married him and had three sons James, Howard and Joe. We moved away from Goose Gap when the boys were young to Seymour, Tennessee, stayed there until the boys were all married and Bethel was ready for retirement. Seymour had been a good place to live and neighbors were the best. They became like family and will remain like that until death. But Bethel wanted to come back to Goose Gap "Home" he called it. He could look out ahead and see what was best. My oldest sister had passed away and in three months my mom died and I could see I needed my brothers and sisters to help me on through life.

I know Seymour will always be a special place in our son's hearts, but I think they can see now that it was best that we come back to Goose Gap to our family and friends and the Church, Mountain View, which was built when I was four years old and I have been associated with all my life. I was saved there at an early age. Our boys helped us build our house on Goose Gap Road just like I wanted it.

I am thankful for my life and hope I can live it and not be a reproach on any of my family, my church or my friends.

**The grass withereth
the flower fadeth:
but the word of our God
shall stand for ever.**
KJV

www.ingramcontent.com/pod-product-compliance
Lightning Source LLC
Chambersburg PA
CBHW050907260726
48660CB00001B/68

9 781979 105248